2006

D1478426

Culture and Customs
of Liberia

Liberia. Cartography by Bookcomp.

Culture and Customs of Liberia

∽∘∾

AYODEJI OLUKOJU

Culture and Customs of Africa
Toyin Falola, Series Editor

GREENWOOD PRESS
Westport, Connecticut • London

Library of Congress Cataloging-in-Publication Data

Olukoju, Ayodeji.
   Culture and customs of Liberia / Ayodeji Olukoju.
      p. cm. — (Culture and customs of Africa, ISSN 1530–8367)
   Includes bibliographical references and index.
   ISBN 0–313–33291–6 (alk. paper)
   1. Liberia—Social life and customs. 2. Liberia—Civilization.
I. Title. II. Series.
DT629.O45 2006
966.62—dc22   2005030569

British Library Cataloguing in Publication Data is available.

Library of Congress Catalog Card Number: 2005030569
ISBN 0–313–33291–6
ISSN: 1530–8367

First published in 2006

Greenwood Press, 88 Post Road West, Westport, CT 06881
An imprint of Greenwood Publishing Group, Inc.
www.greenwood.com

Printed in the United States of America

The paper used in this book complies with the
Permanent Paper Standard issued by the National
Information Standards Organization (Z39.48–1984).

10 9 8 7 6 5 4 3 2 1

Copyright Acknowledgments

The author and publisher gratefully acknowledge permission to reprint the following:

Song lyrics from the Liberian Studies Journal, "Categories of Traditional Liberian Songs" by Moore and
"Bai T. Moore's Poetry…" by Ofri-Scheps. Reprinted with permission of Liberian Studies Journal via
Copyright Clearance Center.

In loving memory of my beloved grandparents:
Naomi and Emmanuel Olukoju, of Iroho, Okia, Oka-Akoko and
Ibitola and John Odole, of Iyayu, Idoani

Contents

Series Foreword		ix
Preface		xi
Acknowledgments		xiii
Chronology		xv
1	Introduction	1
2	Religion and Worldview	21
3	Literature and Media	41
4	Art, Architecture, and Housing	59
5	Cuisine and Traditional Dress	79
6	Gender Roles, Marriage, and Family	91
7	Social Customs and Lifestyle	109
8	Music and Dance	127
Glossary		147
Index		151

Series Foreword

AFRICA is a vast continent, the second largest, after Asia. It is four times the size of the United States, excluding Alaska. It is the cradle of human civilization. A diverse continent, Africa has more than fifty countries with a population of over 700 million people who speak over 1,000 languages. Ecological and cultural differences vary from one region to another. As an old continent, Africa is one of the richest in culture and customs, and its contributions to world civilization are impressive indeed.

Africans regard culture as essential to their lives and future development. Culture embodies their philosophy, worldview, behavior patterns, arts, and institutions. The books in this series intend to capture the comprehensiveness of African culture and customs, dwelling on such important aspects as religion, worldview, literature, media, art, housing, architecture, cuisine, traditional dress, gender, marriage, family, lifestyles, social customs, music, and dance.

The uses and definitions of "culture" vary, reflecting its prestigious association with civilization and social status, its restriction to attitude and behavior, its globalization, and the debates surrounding issues of tradition, modernity, and postmodernity. The participating authors have chosen a comprehensive meaning of culture while not ignoring the alternative uses of the term.

Each volume in the series focuses on a single country, and the format is uniform. The first chapter presents a historical overview, in addition to information on geography, economy, and politics. Each volume then proceeds to examine the various aspects of culture and customs. The series highlights the mechanisms for the transmission of tradition and culture across generations: the

significance of orality, traditions, kinship rites, and family property distribution; the rise of print culture; and the impact of educational institutions. The
series also explores the intersections between local, regional, national, and
global bases for identity and social relations. While the volumes are organized
nationally, they pay attention to ethnicity and language groups and the links
between Africa and the wider world.

The books in the series capture the elements of continuity and change in
culture and customs. Custom is not represented as static or as a museum arti-
fact, but as a dynamic phenomenon. Furthermore, the authors recognize the
current challenges to traditional wisdom, which include gender relations; the
negotiation of local identities in relation to the state; the significance of struggles for power at national and local levels and their impact on cultural traditions
and community-based forms of authority; and the tensions between agrarian
and industrial/manufacturing/oil-based economic modes of production.

Africa is a continent of great changes, instigated mainly by Africans but
also through influences from other continents. The rise of youth culture, the
penetration of the global media, and the challenges to generational stability
are some of the components of modern changes explored in the series. The
ways in which traditional (non-Western and nonimitative) African cultural
forms continue to survive and thrive, that is, how they have taken advantage
of the market system to enchance their influence and reproductions, also
receive attention.

Through the books in this series, readers can see their own cultures in a
different perspective, understand the habits of Africans, and educate themselves about the customs and cultures of other countries and people. The
hope is that the readers will come to respect the cultures of others and see
them not as inferior or superior to theirs, but merely as different. Africa has
always been important to Europe and the United States, essentially as a source
of labor, raw materials, and markets. Blacks are in Europe and the Americas
as part of the African diaspora, a migration that took place primarily because
of the slave trade. Recent African migrants increasingly swell their number
and visibility. It is important to understand the history of the diaspora and
the newer migrants, as well as the roots of the culture and customs of the
places from where they come. It is equally important to understand others in
order to be able to interact successfully in a world that keeps shrinking. The
accessible nature of the books in this series will contribute to this understanding and enhance the quality of human interaction in a new millennium.

Toyin Falola
Frances Higginbothom Nalle Centennial Professor in History
The University of Texas at Austin

Preface

THIS BOOK FOCUSES ON aspects of the culture and customs of Liberia: indigenous and externally derived religious practices; literature and media; art and architecture; dress and food culture; family, gender, and marriage practices; social customs and lifestyle; and music and dance. Much attention is paid to continuity and change in lifestyle and cultural forms, and the agents and direction of change. The numerically insignificant Americo-Liberians and descendants of liberated slaves played a disproportionately great role in the evolution of several aspects of Liberian culture, including dress, cuisine, Christian religious practices, Western-style marriage customs, and Western literacy. The blend of the indigenous and foreign has thus produced a Liberian culture that is heavily influenced by Western (especially American) ideas.

Yet many indigenous elements, including secret societies such as the Poro and Sande, have survived the Western impact and have continued to play some role in the development of Liberian society. As well, political turbulence in the country since the 1980 coup has traumatized the peoples of Liberia, generating forced population movements that brought many diverse peoples together. The conflict thus indirectly fostered the blend of cultures in places such as Monrovia and other urban centers, and in refugee camps outside the country, where refugees of diverse origins have had to interact at close range.

English serves as the lingua franca, a heritage of American involvement in the establishment of the Liberian colony in the nineteenth century. However, even that foreign language has come to terms with local usage, reflected in the varieties of English, including Standard Liberian English and pidgin. In spite of efforts of various ethnic groups to promote group identity in Liberia and the diaspora, English in its various forms continues to be the dominant medium of official and business transactions, especially in government service and schools. This is especially so given that there is no clearly dominant ethnic group with a language spoken by a sizable proportion of the population. Yet the early invention of various indigenous scripts, such as the Vai script, illustrates how the stimulus provided by Islamic and Western literacy has aided indigenous literacy.

Liberian music has likewise exemplified the blend of the indigenous and the foreign. Employing local and foreign instruments and lyrics, brands of music often representing an amalgam of the indigenous and foreign elements have since flourished in the country and been exported overseas. Liberian dance forms reflect the different cultures of the country's ethnic groups. While some are purely secular, others are exclusive to secret societies such as Poro and Sande. Like music, language, and education, Liberian cuisine and dress have indigenous and foreign components, as is the case in most other West African countries. Urbanization, especially in prewar Liberia, aided the development of leisure and the arts in general. It may be argued that cultural borrowing in such contexts, much more than political integration, has ensured a sense of Liberian cultural identity.

Still, one should be careful not to exaggerate the cultural unity of Liberia in that striking differences still exist and have probably been accentuated in some cases by the political developments of the last two decades. However, the division is no longer that between the so-called civilized settlers and their native counterparts from the hinterland provinces. But the cultural influence of the former subsists even though they lost power in 1980 and represent less than 5 percent of the total population.

Acknowledgments

THE CHALLENGE TO write this book was thrown at me by the series editor, Toyin Falola, and it is to him I owe my greatest debt of gratitude for the opportunity to undertake the task of writing this book. I also gratefully acknowledge the encouraging support and comments of my indefatigable editor, Wendi Schnaufer, who patiently endured my delayed takeoff and added wind to my sail with her speedy processing of my chapters as they tumbled in, and Apex Publishing and Linda Ellis-Stiewing of Greenwood Press for editorial and sundry assistance.

I am grateful to those who assisted in the collection of data: Lisa Lindsay of the University of North Carolina at Chapel Hill; Patrick Mbajekwe of Old Dominion University, Norfolk, Va.; Jeremiah Dibua of Morgan State University, Baltimore; Olutayo Adesina, then Rhodes Fellow at Oxford University; Hakeem Tijani, then of Henderson State University, Arkadelphia; and Kristin Mann and John "Thabiti" Willis of Emory University, Atlanta. Nothing could have been achieved without the immense support offered by these great friends.

I must acknowledge the indispensable support of various institutions and colleagues that afforded me the time and space to collect data and to write the manuscript: my employers, the University of Lagos, Akoka-Yaba, Lagos, Nigeria, for granting me a yearlong sabbatical leave; the Institute of African Studies and the Department of History, Emory University, Atlanta (and my kind hosts, Kristin Mann and Edna Bay), for a grant and affiliation, including access to their library; and the Deutscher Akademischer Austauschdienst

(DAAD) for offering me a three-month fellowship tenable at the Johannes Gutenberg Universitat, Mainz, Germany. I am deeply grateful to Dr. Roland Weiss and, especially, Professor Dr. Thomas Bierschenk for facilitating the award, and to the latter for ensuring my affiliation with his institute. The superb collection of the institute's library yielded valuable data for this book while I was working on another project. I have also received advice and tangible assistance from Professor Alpha Bah of the College of Charleston, South Carolina, and from the Salau-Okelejis—Ahmed, Aderonke, and their children—my wonderful hosts in Lawrenceville, Georgia, where I did a good proportion of data collection and writing.

I am, as usual, deeply grateful to members of my family, especially my ever-supportive wife, Omowumi, and our children—Oluwadamilola, Omolola, Oreoluwa, and Oluwaseyi—for bearing with my absence while I worked on this book project. Finally, I thank God for sparing my life and for blessing all my endeavours with success.

Chronology

1815	African American Quaker and maritime entrepreneur Paul Cuffee (or Cuffe) finances and captains a successful voyage to Sierra Leone, where he helps a small group of African American immigrants establish themselves.
1817	The partial success of Paul Cuffee's African venture encourages white proponents of colonization to form an organization to repatriate free African Americans who wish to settle in Africa.
1820	The American Colonization Society (ACS) sends its first group of immigrants to Sherbro Island in Sierra Leone.
1821	The ACS dispatches a representative, Dr. Eli Ayres, to purchase land farther north up the coast from Sierra Leone.
1822	The survivors of Sherbro Island arrive at Cape Mesurado on April 25 and establish a settlement.
1824	A few armed settlers expel the ACS representative following complaints of unfair allocation of land and provisions. Ashmun (a Methodist missionary, who replaced Ayres as the representative of ACS)

later returns after the reconciliation. The settlement originally called Christopolis is renamed Monrovia after the American president, James Monroe, and the entire colony is named Liberia.

1827   Slave states in North America encourage the formation of colonization societies to get rid of the free African American population. Operating independently of the ACS, they promote the colonization of Liberia. Slaves are emancipated on the condition that they emigrate. Maryland, Virginia, and Mississippi establish colonies in Liberia for former slaves and free blacks.

1838   A merger of the colonies is established by the Virginia Colonization Society, the Quaker Young Men's Colonization Society of Pennsylvania, and the American Colonization Society to form the Commonwealth of Liberia. Joseph Jenkins Roberts, a trader and successful military commander from Virginia, is named the first lieutenant governor. Following the death in 1841 of the governor, he becomes the first African American governor of the colony.

1842   The Mississippi settlement on the Sinoe River joins the Commonwealth.

1846   Americo-Liberians vote for independence.

1847   The Liberian Declaration of Independence is adopted and signed on July 26.

1848   The Liberian constitution is ratified; former governor J. J. Roberts emerges as Liberia's first elected president.

1851   Liberia College is founded.

1854   Maryland Colony, located between the Grand Cess and San Pedro rivers, declares its independence from the Maryland State Colonization Society.

1857   Maryland Colony becomes a county of Liberia.

1862	President Abraham Lincoln accords official diplomatic recognition to Liberia.
1865	An influx of 346 immigrants comes from Barbados and the United States after the American Civil War.
1868	The Liberian government asserts limited control over the hinterland.
1869	The True Whig Party, which held on to power from the late nineteenth century to 1980, is founded.
1871	A high-interest bank loan scandal leads to President Edward J. Roye's removal from office.
1875	The United States lends naval support to the Republic of Liberia in its war with the Grebo (a southern Liberian indigenous people).
1883	Liberia loses the Gallinas (a territory named after the Gallinas River) to the British colony of Sierra Leone.
1888	Edward W. Blyden's *Christianity, Islam and the Negro Race* is published.
1892	France seizes territory between the Cavalla and San Pedro rivers.
1903	The border is demarcated between Liberia and the British colony of Sierra Leone.
1904	The Liberian government institutes indirect rule in the hinterland.
1919	Liberia signs the League of Nations covenant.
1929	In the famous Fernando Po scandal, the League of Nations investigates charges of slavery and forced labor in Liberia.
1944	William V. S. Tubman is elected president of Liberia.
1946	Suffrage is extended to Liberia's indigenous peoples.
1958	Liberian representatives attend the first conference of independent African nations.

1967	Liberian officials serve on the Organization of African Unity's Consultation Committee on Nigeria's civil war.
1971	President William V. S. Tubman dies in office and is succeeded by his vice president, William R. Tolbert Jr.
1972	Tolbert is formally elected president.
1979	Bloody riots follow a rally on April 14 against higher rice prices.
1980	Samuel Kanyon Doe and his fellow indigenous Liberian noncommissioned officers assassinate President Tolbert in a bloody coup.
1985	Doe is elected civilian president in controversial elections.
1986	A new constitution inaugurates Liberia's second republic.
1989	Charles Taylor, an Americo-Liberian fugitive from the law, makes an armed incursion into Liberia, which begins a protracted political upheaval characterized by the emergence of competing armed militias with foreign backing.
1990	President Samuel Doe is abducted and executed by forces of Prince Yormie Johnson.
1995	The Economic Community of West African States (ECOWAS), which had sent an interventionist force (called ECOMOG) into the war-ravaged country, secures a truce among Liberia's warring factions. An interim State Council is constituted to prepare the country for elections.
1997	Charles Taylor, the most successful of the warlords, is elected president of Liberia's third republic.
1999	Civil war breaks out in Liberia.
2003	Charles Taylor is exiled to Nigeria. An interim government, headed by Charles Gyude Bryant, is established.

2005   Presidential elections in October usher in another Republic. Former soccer star, George Weah, is front-runner but loses the run-off election to Ellen Johnson-Sirleaf, Liberia's and Africa's first elected female president.

1

Introduction

The love of liberty brought us here.

—Liberian national motto, 1847

THE YEAR 1997 MARKED the 150th anniversary of independence for the
Republic of Liberia, a nation with a unique history. In 1822, the American
Colonization Society founded Liberia as a colony for free African Americans—
a striking instance in which a social conflict in the United States led to mass
emigration to another continent. Hence, the name Liberia, derived from the
Latin, *liber*, meaning "free," was given to the colony. In 1847 the repatriates
declared their independence from the Society, thus launching the first republic in Africa and, after Haiti, the second modern black state. With citizenship
since 1847 having been limited by law to people of African descent, Liberians
consist of various admixtures of Africans indigenous to the area; descendants
of Ibo and Congolese who were settled there after being liberated from slave
ships in the nineteenth century; and black immigrants from the United States,
the Caribbean, and other parts of Africa. After a long period of relative stability and peace, the country descended into a brutal and anarchic civil war that
lasted from December 1989 to July 1997. The high level of violence and ten-
sion waned with the inauguration in August 1997 of a new government based
on the elections held a month earlier under the supervision of the international community.

Although Liberia had existed as an independent African nation and a symbol of hope to the African peoples under the rule of various colonial powers,
its recent history has been bedeviled by a prolonged upheaval following the

military coup d'état of 1980. First, that event ended the more than one hundred years of nonindigenous (Americo-Liberian) rule. Second, it dented the country's image of a stable polity, and the Doe regime rapidly degenerated into an unmitigated autocracy that plunged the nation into a ruinous seven year war that ended only in 1997. Meanwhile, the Liberian war had assumed regional and international dimensions, culminating in the intervention of the Economic Community of West Africa (ECOWAS), whose intervention force, known as ECOMOG (ECOWAS Monitoring Group), played a critical role in the events leading to the final resolution. Although ECOMOG was a regional initiative, its fighting force was constituted by Nigeria, Ghana, and Guinea, with Nigeria bearing the brunt of the funding, fighting, and casualties.

Following the capture and brutal murder of Doe by forces of Yormie Johnson, a transitional government headed by an intellectual, Amos Sawyer, was installed to prepare the way for democratic elections. Already, forces of Charles Ghankay Taylor, leader of the National Patriotic Front of Liberia (NPLF), had overrun virtually all of the country, and the capture of Monrovia had been forestalled only by the presence of ECOMOG. Ultimately, the fighting forces of the different factions were disarmed, and democratic elections were held that ushered in the government of Charles Taylor, undisputed victor in the elections. Another cycle of revolt and instability was provoked by Taylor's style of government and his involvement in, and escalation of, another savage war in neighboring Sierra Leone.

The United Nations then imposed sanctions on the government of President Taylor given his involvement in, and the escalation of, that conflict. He was accused of offering material and military support to Foday Sankoh, leader of the Revolutionary United Front (RUF), a ruthless group that gained international infamy for cutting off the limbs of its opponents, especially defenseless women and children; raping and killing women; and pressing child soldiers into its army. The UN banned the export of Liberian diamonds and travel by Liberian government officials. At the same time, opposition forces were also seizing large parts of the country, as Taylor himself had done on his way to power. Taylor was finally persuaded to go into exile in Nigeria, where he still resides awaiting trial in the face of his indictment for war crimes in Sierra Leone.

LAND

The Republic of Liberia is located on the windward coast of West Africa. Covering a total of 43,000 square miles, it is bordered by the Atlantic Ocean to the south, Sierra Leone and Guinea to the west and north, and Côte D'Ivoire to the east. It has a coastline of 360 miles (579 kilometers) and land frontiers of 445, 350, and 190 miles (716, 563, and 306 kilometers), respectively, with Guinea, Côte D'Ivoire, and Sierra Leone. The land consists of rolling plateau and low mountains in the northeast, and flat or rolling coastal plains. Mount Wuteve is the highest peak at 4,528 feet (1,380 meters) above sea level. The vegetation varies from the mangrove trees of the coastal swamps to the grasslands and tropical forest of the hinterland. The weather is hot and humid; there are frequent showers in summer and hot days and cold nights in winter. There are two distinct seasons: dry season from November to April, and wet season from May to October. Annual rainfall averages 180 inches along the coast and 70 inches in the hinterland, the bulk of which falls between April and November.

Liberia is endowed with such natural resources as diamonds, iron ore, timber, and gold, in addition to hydropower. According to a 1998 estimate, only 2 percent of the land area is devoted to each of permanent crops and arable farming; the rest (over 95 percent) is committed to a variety of other uses. These activities, especially slash-and-burn agriculture and logging, have caused considerable damage to the environment in terms of deforestation, soil erosion, and loss of biodiversity. As laterization is the predominant process of soil formation, the soils of Liberia sustain the cultivation of permanent crops as well as arable crops, though they are also prone to degradation and erosion. Consequently, the natural conditions favor permanent crops like tree crops more than arable crops and pastures, which require special efforts to maintain soil fertility.

PEOPLES

Liberia is peopled by a multiplicity of ethnic groups speaking various indigenous languages and English. The total population of 3,288,198 (2002 estimates) comprises the indigenous ethnic groups, which constitute 95 percent of the population, and the Congo people, descendants of resettled former slaves from the New World, who account for just over 2 percent of the total. The indigenous ethnic groups include the Bassa, Gio, Kpelle, Vai, Loma, Kissi, Gola, Gbandi, Dei, Krahn, Belle, Mende, Mandingo, Grebo, Mano, and Kru. The Kru is a renowned maritime group that supplied the bulk of the labor force on European ships up to the mid-twentieth century. It would appear that the oldest inhabitants of the Liberian area are the Gola, Kpelle, Loma, Gbandi, Mende, and Mano. These groups had settled in the area by about 6000 B.C. By the sixteenth century, some other groups migrated from the direction of modern Côte D'Ivoire to the east. Among these were the Kru, Bassa, Dei, and Grebo. During the following century still others moved into the territory of modern Liberia from the northern direction: the

Vai and Mandingo belong to this category. The fourth set of arrivals were the Americo-Liberians, freed slaves or their descendants from the New World (the United States and the Caribbean), and the Congo people, presumably from the Congo Basin, the recaptives who had been rescued before actually being exported out of the region. These were transplants from outside the immediate vicinity who, unlike the Americo-Liberians, were not yet exposed to New World slavery.

LANGUAGES

Located at the terminus of four major West African language groups, Liberia has as many as twenty discrete indigenous languages in use. Many of these have dialectal variations. Thus, there are two variations of the Krahn language: Eastern and Western Krahn. Western Krahn is spoken in parts of Côte d'Ivoire and Liberia. According to 1991 and 1993 research, there are an estimated 47,800 Western Krahn speakers in Liberia and 12,200 in Côte d'Ivoire.

Many of the indigenous languages of Liberia have made the transition to written form. A notable example is the Vai script, which is renowned as an indigenous African invention. While the Vai, Bassa, Kpelle, and Loma languages developed local scripts, Vai also evolved its own literature. English is the official language. Although only an estimated 20 percent of the population employ English in official business, the language has been domesticated as in other parts of the world. This is in the form of pidgin, a language of commerce and urban life in West Africa. The Creole form of English, known as Liberian English, serves as an unofficial lingua franca. However, the use of English is widespread, resulting from the manner of the establishment of the country, the impact of the media, and increasing literacy rates.

EDUCATION

As in other parts of Africa, education in Liberia is a blend of the indigenous and Western. Indigenous apprenticeship in crafts, the guild system, and other informal systems of education complement the formal school system. Given its origin as an outpost of the United States, Liberia had a head start in formal (Western) education in the nineteenth century. The leading higher institutions are Cuttington College in Harper and the University of Liberia in Monrovia. The University of Liberia was established in 1862 as Liberia College, having been incorporated by an act of Parliament in December 1851. The charter merged its constituent divisions—the College of Liberal and Fine Arts (at Liberia College) and the William V. S. Tubman Teacher College. Eventually, in 1951, it became a full-fledged university, the first degree-awarding institution in West Africa. Cuttington College, the oldest private coeducational four-year degree-awarding institution in sub-Saharan Africa, was founded in 1889 with a grant of $5,000 from Robert Fulton Cutting. A treasurer of the Episcopal Church in the United States, Cutting desired the establishment of a "manual labor farm" for boys in the Mission schools. The Divinity School began at Cape Palmas in 1897 and was named Cuttington Collegiate and Divinity School in honor of Cutting. For the next 40 years, the school produced a stream of graduates in classical education, but it closed in 1929 as a result of financial constraints. It was resuscitated in 1949 on a 1,500-acre parcel of land at Suacoco, Bong County, 120 miles north of Monrovia, and subsequently developed into five degree-awarding institutions in education, the humanities, natural science, nursing, and theology. Cuttington College was closed between 1990 and 1997 during the Liberian civil war, but it has since reopened fully, though the scars of war remain.

CITIES

Most Liberians live in modest town and villages, especially in the counties and provinces outside the capital city of Monrovia. The other major settlements are Buchanan, Gbarnga, Greenville, Harper, Roberstsport, Sanniquellie, Tubmanburg, and Yekepa. Monrovia, with a current estimated population of 1.3 million, is the capital city and the leading administrative, commercial, and financial center. Established in 1822, Monrovia was named after President James Monroe of the United States. Located on a peninsula between the Atlantic Ocean and the Mesurado River, the city developed out of an initial settlement established on Providence Island by the American Colonization Society, which supported the emigration of Americo-Liberians to Africa. The city of Monrovia has a harbor that was developed during World War II as an American base. Industries operating in the vicinity of the harbor include the production of food products, cement, refined petroleum, and chemicals. Monrovia is also a cultural and educational center, containing the national museum, a zoo, and higher-education institutions such as the University of Liberia. Like most other Liberian cities, Monrovia was severely affected by the civil wars of the 1990s. It was particularly devastated by the pitched battles between the forces of President Samuel Doe and those of Prince Yormie Johnson in 1990, and a major assault by the forces of Charles Taylor in 1992.

Buchanan, Liberia's second largest port, named after U.S. president James Buchanan (1857–61), is located on Waterhouse Bay, east of Monrovia. It is the capital of Grand Bassa County. Unlike other Liberian cities, it was spared the ravages of the Liberian civil war. Greenville, also known as Sinoe, is the

capital of Sinoe County. Located on the lagoon near the Sinoe River and the
Atlantic Ocean, it was largely destroyed during the war but has been rebuilt
to some extent. Its port serves as the outlet for the local logging industry.
Harper, or Cape Palmas, capital of Maryland County, is an important administrative center and home to Cuttington College, the oldest private tertiary
institution in Liberia. The town and the college were destroyed during the
war, but both have been rebuilt substantially. Fishing is the main industry of
the community. Tubmanburg, also known as Bomi, is the capital of Bomi
County to the north of Monrovia. An important diamond and iron ore mining center, it was a flashpoint during the war and was, accordingly, largely
destroyed during the conflict. It was the headquarters of the Liberians United
for Reconciliation and Democracy (LURD) militia. Gbarnga, in Bong
County northeast of the capital, served as Charles Taylor's base during the
war, while Sanniquellie in northern Liberia achieved renown for hosting the
talks among presidents Tubman of Liberia, Nkrumah of Ghana, and Sekou
Toure of Guinea preparatory to the formation of the Organization of African
Unity in 1963. Roberstport in western Liberia, a World War II Allied subma-
rine base, is a major seaside resort notable for its surfing and fishing. It too
was devastated by the Liberian civil war. Yekepa, in northern Liberia close to
the border with Guinea, was a base for the Lamco iron mining company and
was another victim of the war.

By African standards, these are modest settlements, though their fortunes
have also been affected by the protracted civil war of the 1990s. Monrovia

Monrovia, Liberia, Broad Street in the city center. © Topham/
The Image Works.

was and remains the most important political, cultural, and economic center in Liberia. Most of the Liberian cities and towns are currently recovering from the physical damage and trauma inflicted by the war.

RESOURCES, OCCUPATIONS, AND ECONOMY

Liberia is endowed with considerable human, physical, and natural resources. Among these are gold, hydropower, rubber (Liberia being the sixth-largest world producer and the largest in Africa), coffee, cocoa, cassava, palm oil, rice (the main staple of most Liberians), sugarcane, bananas, timber, and livestock. The country's exports are iron ore (the major foreign exchange earner), gold, diamonds, cocoa, coffee, timber, rubber, and small quantities of bauxite and columbite. Imports include manufactured goods, chemicals, fuels, machinery, transport equipment, rice, and other foodstuffs. The industrial sector is dominated by foreign-owned manufacturing industries, mainly rubber and oil palm processing. Agriculture alone was responsible for 60 percent of the GDP, while industry and services accounted for 10 and 30 percent, respectively, in 2001. The employment of the labor force also followed the same pattern. According to a 2000 estimate, agriculture, industry, and services employ 70, 8, and 22 percent, respectively, of the Liberian workforce.

The country is also renowned for its maritime registry, which comprises its flag-of-convenience fleet. Although the great bulk of the fleet is not owned by Liberia, it confers on the country the status of a leading power in the world's

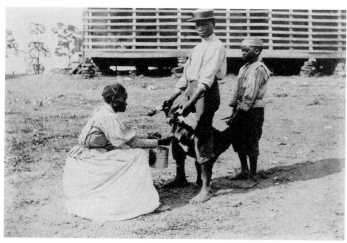

Method of goat milking. Courtesy of the Library of Congress.

mercantile marine industry. By 2002, it was estimated that the Liberian fleet consisted of 1,513 ships of 1,000 GRT (gross registered tonnage) and over, totaling 51,912,244 GRT/79,297,046 DWT (deadweight tons).

The civil war of the 1990s inflicted great damage on Liberia's infrastructure. By 1989, there were three rail systems owned and operated by foreign steel and financial interests in conjunction with the Liberian government. However, the Lamco Railroad closed in 1989 when iron ore production ceased, and the others were forced to halt operations by the civil war. Large sections of the rail track were subsequently dismantled and sold for scrap in 2001.

GOVERNMENT

Until the military coup of 1980, Liberia had been Africa's oldest republic. The transmutation of Master Sergeant Samuel Doe to an elected president in 1985 restored Liberia to a semblance of democratic rule, though the elections were brazenly manipulated to ensure Doe's victory. A new constitution came into effect on January 6, 1986. The election of Charles Taylor as president inaugurated another attempt at constitutional government, but this was aborted by another round of political turbulence. However, the constitutional arrangements remained, based on the American model. The government comprises three arms: the executive, the legislature, and the judiciary. The president, who combines the offices of chief of state and head of government, is elected by popular vote for a renewable term of six years. He is assisted by the vice president, elected on the same ballot, and his cabinet, whose appointments by the president are subject to Senate ratification. The National Assembly or legislature is bicameral, consisting of the Senate and the House of Representatives. The former consists of 26 members who are elected by popular vote for a nine-year term, while the latter has 64 members whose tenure is for six years. The judiciary, headed by the chief justice, administers a blend of Western (Anglo-Saxon or American) and indigenous legal traditions.

HISTORY

Prelude to Modern Liberia: Developments to c. 1800

Although limited, archaeology and oral traditions reveal a record of human habitation in the geographical area now known as Liberia that can be traced to antiquity. Although precise dates cannot be given, there is some evidence that the area may have been occupied during the Sangoan period of the Stone Age.

These earliest settlers are presumed to have been hunters and gatherers, possibly with some rudimentary forms of root horticulture. They probably were a part of the large Niger-Congo-speaking peoples that populates much of West Africa to this day, and the earliest group in the Liberian area probably spoke a form of what today is classified as the Mel languages, represented by the Kissi and Gola. In the eastern section of Liberia, the area inhabited by Kruan-speaking peoples (Dei, Kuwaa [Belle], Bassa, Wee [Kran], Kru, and Grebo), there is evidence of a general westward-southwestward movement of these peoples and of their linguistic and ethnic similarities to peoples in western Côte d'Ivoire. In addition, a branch of these people, the Dei, reached as far as the mouth of the Mano River, on Liberia's western boundary, prior to 1500. Linguistic evidence also supports the westward spread of the Kuwaa (Belle) just to the interior of the Dei.

The third major population, which settled in Liberia after the Mel and Kruan speakers, was the Mande-speaking peoples, who seem to have moved out of the western savannah and into the forest region. Within Liberia there are three branches of the Mande language family. The Ma (Mano) and Dan (Gio), speakers of the southern subdivision of Mande, were probably the earliest groups to penetrate and settle in the forest region. The second Mande-speaking group to enter this region was the southwestern subdivision of Mande speakers represented today by the Kpelle, Loma, Bandi, and Mende. The third group of Mande speakers is the Vai, a part of the northern Mande subdivision. Their migration may be dated to about 1500, when they reached the coast in the area of the Mano River. The cultivation of grains, particularly rice, has been brought by migrations of Mande-speaking people from the savannah region. It is possible that this latter group also brought the techniques of spinning and weaving as well as the ability to work metal, particularly to smelt iron. A major nexus for articulation of various ethnic groups and polities was the secret societies found throughout the northwest region. These societies, responsible for training youths in various artisan and other pursuits, were organized into male lodges, known generally as Poro, and female societies, called Sande. In addition to their educational role, the societies mediated between various polities during times of conflict and controlled the supply of iron money. The dominance of specialists in these societies is reflected in the use of the same word, *zo* or *zoo,* for both high officials of the male societies and highly qualified artisans.

Indigenous institutions, like the chieftaincy and Poro, were severely strained by several centuries of slave trading. The common people (especially in the interior) were as victimized by the trade as their rulers (particularly on the coast) were dependent on it for the guns and jewelry that ensured their prestige. In the nineteenth century, the slave trade would decline because it both became economically untenable and was opposed by a growing abolitionist movement in Europe and the United States. After Britain abolished the slave trade in 1807, efforts by the Royal Navy to drive slavers from other more frequented markets merely increased the traffic on this coast. However, opposition to the slave trade in the early nineteenth century provided the basis for a consensus between repatriates and those indigenous Africans who had been victimized by the trade.

The American Colonization Society and the Establishment of the Liberian Colony, 1816–47

Beginning in 1816, the American Colonization Society (ACS), supported by such leading Americans as senators Henry Clay and Daniel Webster and presidents Thomas Jefferson, James Madison, and James Monroe, worked toward the creation of a colony in Africa for free blacks and manumitted slaves, along the lines of an earlier British effort at Sierra Leone. Implementation of the joint venture began after the U.S. Congress granted $100,000 for the repatriation to Africa of persons brought to America following the official American abolition of the slave trade. Between 1822 and 1867, the ACS succeeded in assisting the repatriation to Liberia of 19,000 black people, among them 4,540 freeborn, 7,000 manumitted slaves, and more than 5,700 recaptured from slaving vessels.

The ACS experiment itself was of historic significance. A group whose ancestors had been exiled from Africa had now returned to the land of their roots, to a country populated by many other African peoples. For repatriates, their return had been motivated in part by the desire for liberty, defined largely as the opportunity to enjoy what they had been denied in America, particularly property ownership and their own institutions. The transplant of the black repatriates on the Liberian coast coincided with a pattern that had been charted by groups like the Vai before them and that would be followed later by some Mandingo, as an initial group of traders and missionaries were later joined by other kinfolk. Their path was paved in part by the prestige already conferred upon them by their religion and their larger trade networks.

The first settlement by black New World repatriates in the area now known as Liberia was at Cape Mesurado, which was ceded in 1821 to agents of the ACS by the leaders of several ethnic groups then living in the area, specifically the Dei, Gola, and Bassa. It may be noted that relations with the indigenous peoples deteriorated after the establishment of the colony, and the indigenous peoples made unsuccessful attempts to destroy the colony. That settlement evolved into what is now Monrovia, the capital city. Some of the institutions created by immigrants, such as their families and religious ceremonies, were part African, providing a further basis for articulation with indigenous Africans.

Others, such as the political construction of the Liberian state, were fundamentally informed by the nonindigenous background of the repatriates. Still others, such as the press and features of the bureaucratic state, were without significant antecedents in repatriate and indigenous cultures and, initially at least, would be operated by self-conscious recourse to explicitly articulated rules. The administrative division of the modern Liberian state has evolved over more than a century and a half of existence from dispersed indigenous communities and coastal settlement/hinterland regions through counties and provinces to the present 13 counties.

Independent Liberia to 1944

For most of the nineteenth century, the authority of the Liberian government was confined to a few scattered coastal towns that were inhabited mainly by the repatriates and their descendants, with the rest of what is now Liberian territory occupied by separate polities inhabited by indigenes and governed by traditional rulers. The noncontinuous nature of the early Liberian polity, although an anomaly by Western standards, was relatively common in the West African forest belt, where the dense tropical vegetation made communication difficult even between relatively proximal settlements. Commercial, political, and military reasons prompted expansion, which proceeded along the coast until 1857, when the formation of coastal Liberia was virtually complete with four of the five coastal counties, namely, Montserrado, Grand Bassa, Sinoe, and Maryland. The impetus for significant expansion into the hinterland was provided by the 1884–85 Berlin African Congress, at which European imperialists mandated that countries at the conference demonstrate effective territorial occupation of lands claimed. Trade imperatives also spurred movement into the interior. Inland expansion helped to erase an earlier distinction between the first counties, which had a width not exceeding 40 miles from the coast, and the adjoining territory, which in 1869 became known as the hinterland.

Only in the twentieth century, therefore, was the state consolidated into its current form, encompassing an area of about 37,743 square miles. This geographic expansion of the polity produced a population increase, from 45,000 around 1900 to about one million in 1930. It also engendered conflicts with indigenous peoples, such as with the Grebo (1857, 1875, and 1910), the Kru (1915–1916 and 1930s) and the Gola (1917), to name a few. To enforce the de jure limits of the state, Liberia in 1908 for the first time created a national army, the Liberian Frontier Force. By the first quarter of the twentieth century the hinterland was administratively divided into western, central, and eastern provinces. Liberia thus consisted of five coastal counties (Grand Cape

Mount was created from Montserrado), four territories—Marshall, River Cess, Sasstown, and Kru Coast—incorporated within four counties, and three provinces. The county jurisdiction, inhabited by a smaller percentage of the population (largely of repatriate descent), came under the authority of the statute law system based on the 1847 constitution, but the hinterland (later, provincial) jurisdiction, where the vast majority of the population lived, did not. Not only did this allow for the establishment by the government of informal control over these provinces, but the character of that arrangement was such as to leave interior Liberia in a politically subordinate relationship to the coastal areas until recent times.

Early Liberia faced chronic financial problems that further complicated its national life. In response to the industrial capitalism that began to replace the plantation system worldwide, enterprising Liberians resorted to commercial trading. An admirable Liberian shipping fleet developed but was overtaken by international competitors at the end of the 1860s; the main Liberian economic enterprise then shifted to government employment. And, in the absence of productive industry to generate funds for sustenance of the bureaucracy, an era of foreign loans was initiated. The first loan of 1871 led to others in 1906, 1912, and 1926. As collateral for these loans, many at high interest rates, state revenues (largely from customs tariffs) were conceded, and land and product rights were granted. This economic policy led to the era of concession agreements, the most notable being with Firestone in 1926.

However, Liberia had hardly overcome international intrigue, including American high-handedness during the negotiations of the Firestone agreement, when, in 1929, accusations of internal forced labor generated a scandal. The state was censured internationally for complicity in a system that League of Nations commissioners alleged was "hardly distinguishable from slave-raiding and slave trading."[1] The crisis led to the downfall of the administration of President Charles D. B. King (1920–30). To Edwin J. Barclay (1930–44), his successor, fell the task of unraveling the complications, internal and external, of that episode. Those European powers in the League of Nations that sought to abrogate Liberia's independence by advocating mandate status for the republic were thwarted by the contradictions in international relations of the time as well as by the determination of the Barclay government to forestall that possibility. Concerning the issue of governance of Liberia's indigenous population and the complications caused by the League crisis, Barclay was not so fortunate in that some aggrieved indigenous leaders opted to make common cause with external foes of the state. As a consequence, Barclay adopted a more repressive attitude toward all forms of internal dissent.

Liberia under President Tubman, 1944–71

By the time that William V. S. Tubman (1944–71) became president of Liberia, the country's territorial integrity vis-à-vis the ambitions of external powers was no longer in doubt. Under Tubman, relations improved between the Americo-Liberians and the indigenous peoples, with the aim of assimilating the latter in the society fashioned out by the former. The country's foreign policy was pro-West while its open-door economic policy sought to attract foreign investment into the economy. The country, a major producer of rubber, was a beneficiary of the post–World War II primary export boom of the 1950s and 1960s. Following an enactment of 1963, the country was divided into nine counties including four new ones (Grand Gedeh, Bong, Lofa, and Nimba) in the hinterland. The administrative reorganization was part of a process of integrating the indigenous and Americo-Liberian peoples in the country. National integration, though not far-reaching enough, was promoted by the extension of admittedly limited educational facilities to the hinterland beginning in the 1960s. Still, only a tiny percentage of the population directly benefited from literacy and formal education. Universal adult suffrage too was extended to the indigenous Liberians, though this was circumscribed by a property qualification. However, the reforms of the Tubman era were not fundamental. First, they merely established equality of representation between the overwhelming majority of indigenous peoples, numbering some one million persons, and the 30,000 Americo-Liberians. Second, Liberian so-called democracy retained its features of an absolute presidency that outlived the Tubman era. Third, socioeconomic disparity between the two groups of Liberian citizens remained.

End of an Era: The Tolbert Presidency, 1971–80

At the passing of 75-year old President Tubman, his vice president of 19 years, William R. Tolbert Jr., acceded to the presidency by constitutional succession in July 1971. "Speedy" Tolbert came into office with a considerable public service record, though there were initial doubts about his political acumen. But he held out promises of reforms in the areas of national integration, economic development, and self-reliance, encapsulated in the concept of humanistic capitalism and in slogans such as "war against ignorance, disease, and poverty," "from mat to mattresses," and "rally time," with the proclaimed goal of creating a "wholesome functioning society." He committed himself to economic restructuring and diversification, educational and social development, and decentralized planning. He enlisted technocrats from all sections of the Liberian population and the country's political establishment to prosecute what was largely a populist project.

However, he failed to match his rhetoric with action, and his ambitious political, economic, and social restructuring could not survive the contradictions between the forces of change and the defenders of the status quo within his True Whig Party and the Americo-Liberian community, the latter being his traditional constituency. His tenure witnessed the flowering of a new breed of political actors and movements symbolized by the Liberian National Student Union (LINSU), Progressive Alliance of Liberia (PLA), and Movement for Justice in Africa (MOJA), which had been encouraged by his progressive pronouncements. While he dithered in the prosecution of domestic changes in the face of the emerging contradictions at home, Tolbert was much more forthcoming in projecting his progressive credentials on the international scene.

His identification with such tendencies in such bodies as the Organization of African Unity (OAU) and the Non-Aligned Movement (NAM), which generally pursued an independent agenda at the height of the Cold War, did not endear him to the United States. Hence, Tolbert was on shaky ground in domains of domestic and international politics, not least because of his indecision or failure to openly identify with and champion the clamor for overdue sociopolitical change in Liberia. In any case, his was to be the last of the Americo-Liberian absolute presidencies that had ruled the country since independence. He failed to stem the tide of nepotism, corruption, and rivalry among the leading families in Liberia and to redress the inequitable distribution of power and resources.

Liberia since the 1980 Coup

On April 12, 1980, a group of noncommissioned officers of the Armed Forces of Liberia assassinated President Tolbert in the Executive Mansion in a dawn coup d'état. Led by Master-Sergeant Samuel K. Doe, the putschists justified their violent seizure of power on the grounds of "rampant corruption, misuse of public office, and violation of human rights" by the Tolbert government.[2] They then formed a 17-person People's Redemption Council (PRC), headed by Doe. Significantly, the PRC embarked on the summary trial and public execution of 13 leading members of the Tolbert government. Hundreds of highly educated Liberians fled into exile, depleting the country of much-needed technocratic skill. Then the government was wracked by factional conflict, leading to attempted or alleged coups that by 1985 had led to the detention (without trial) of hundreds and the execution of almost one hundred opponents of the Doe regime.

The continuous attrition led to the elimination of most of Doe's fellow conspirators and the emergence of his own brand of brutal dictatorship, characterized by, among other things, a brutal quelling of a protest by students of the University of Liberia in August 1984. As the regime grew worse, it faced internal opposition that was countered by the uncritical support of the Reagan administration in the United States, which saw Doe as an ally in the ongoing cold war. This support was reflected in the steady increase in U.S. aid from a previous maximum of $20 million before 1980 to $91 million in 1985; military aid rose from $1.4 million to $14 million over the same period. Even so, the Doe regime had to yield to pressure for democratization but manipulated the process to its own advantage when Doe himself stood for election as president in 1985. Predictably, Doe prevailed by brazenly rigging the elections of October 15, 1985, which presumably had been won by the Liberia Action Party.

General disillusionment at the seeming impossibility of peaceful, democratic change fueled the abortive coup led by a member of the PRC, General Thomas Quiwonkpa, who was killed along with a large number of real or suspected collaborators, many of them Quiwonkpa's fellow Nimba people. But the repression merely invited a sustained opposition to the regime in the insurgency spearheaded by Charles Taylor, leader of the National Patriotic Front of Liberia (NPFL). The NPFL launched an armed invasion of Nimba county from its base in Côte d'Ivoire on Christmas Eve in 1989, the beginning of a campaign that turned Liberia into a theater of regional conflict. The insurgency was sustained by the large assortment of local and foreign interest groups that had been alienated by the excesses of the Doe regime. Among the foreign members of the anti-Doe coalition were Burkina Faso, Libya, Côte d'Ivoire, and even France. Such strong foreign support and local mass disaffection explain the lightning speed with which the insurgents seized 95 percent of Liberia within seven months, leaving Doe holed up in the executive mansion in Monrovia.

However, regional politics, including the traditional Anglo-French rivalry, soon intervened and prolonged the conflict for more than seven and a half years, from December 1989 to July 1997. The intervention of ECOMOG, which could have aided a quick resolution of the conflict, was soon bogged down by the personal, pecuniary, and strategic considerations of regional and external interests. The United States and the governments of other West African countries (except those that supported the insurgency) were fearful of the likely demonstration effects on the region of a takeover of government by the Liberian insurgents, whose leader had had a controversial, if not dubious, record. Hence, they intervened not only to end the war but also to forestall a military victory for the NPFL. In June 1990, ECOWAS leaders intervened through a mediation committee supported by the Liberian Inter-Faith Mediation Committee.

Its intervention force, made up largely of Nigerian soldiers commanded by a Ghanaian officer, landed in Monrovia on August 24, 1990. After a conference in Banjul, capital of the Gambia, from August 26 to September 1, 1990, ECOWAS then installed the Interim Government of National Unity (IGNU), constituted by civilians and politicians under the presidency of Amos C. Sawyer, an academic.

Meanwhile, a faction of the NPFL had broken away under the leadership of Prince Yormie Johnson to form the Independent National Patriotic Front of Liberia (INPFL). Based at the Monrovia suburb of Caldwell, the INPFL captured Samuel Kanyon Doe while he was visiting the ECOMOG headquarters, and tortured him to death on September 9, 1990. Following Doe's death, the situation became even more complicated with the emergence of groups opposed to Taylor's NPFL. The Movement for the Redemption of Liberian Muslims (MRM) was formed by Mandingo supporters of Doe based in Guinea. It was led by Doe's former information minister, Alhaji G. V. Kromah. The Liberian United Democratic Front (LUDF) was formed in Sierra Leone by former members of the Armed Forces of Liberia. The MRM and LUDF, formed in April 1991, formally merged in October as the United Liberation Movement for Democracy in Liberia (ULIMO).

A turning point in the conflict was a major offensive by the NPLF on October 20, 1992, that aimed to capture Monrovia, the only outstanding target beyond its reach. The attack proved catastrophic, leaving much of the capital city in ruins after ECOMOG repulsed the insurgents with heavy casualties. Over the next two years, militia groups mushroomed with the split of ULIMO into two groups—ULIMO-K and ULIMO-J—headed by Alhaji Kromah and Roosevelt Johnson, respectively—and the emergence of such groups as Lofa Defence Force (LDF), Nimba Defence Force (NDF), Bong Defence Force (BDF), and the Liberia Peace Council. Though none of these groups was a match for the NPLF, they controlled pockets of territories in various parts of Liberia, mainly ethnic enclaves: ULIMO-K in Upper Lofa and Western Bong; ULIMO-J in Lower Lofa, Bomi, and Grand Cape Mount; LPC along the Grand Kru, River Cess, and Sinoe coasts; and the NPLF in parts of Nimba, Margibi, Maryland, and Bong as well as northern Grand Gedeh.

While the conflict raged with no end in sight, regional and international initiatives were undertaken to bring about a negotiated cessation of hostilities. Various international conferences were held in the capitals of Sierra Leone (in June 1990); the Gambia (August 26 to September 1, 1990); Mali (November 28, 1990); and Togo (February 12, 1991); Yamoussoukro, Côte d'Ivoire (July–September 1991); Geneva, Switzerland (July 16, 1993); Cotonou, Benin (July 25, 1993); Akosombo, Ghana (September 12, 1994); Accra,

Ghana (December 21, 1994); and Abuja, Nigeria (July–August 1995). The August 1995 conference in Abuja finally broke the deadlock in that an agreement was hammered out with the following constituents: demobilization and disarmament of militia groups by January 1997, military and other sanctions to enforce compliance, elections in May 1997, and inauguration of an elected government in July 1997.

The agreement produced a caretaker government under the leadership of Ruth S. F. Perry, and elections were duly held on July 19, 1997. The following political parties and their presidential candidates participated in the elections: Progressive People's Party (PPP)—Chea Cheapoo; National Reformation Party (NRP)—Martin M. N. Sheriff; Free Democratic Party (FDP)—Fayah J. Gbollie; Liberia National Union (LINU)—Harry F. Moniba; Unity Party (UP)—Ellen Johnson-Sirleaf; All Liberia Coalition Party (ALCOP)—Alhaji G. V. Kromah; National Patriotic Party (NPP)—Charles Ghankay Taylor; Alliance of Political Parties (Alliance)—Cletus S. Wotorson; Reformation Alliance Party (RAP)— Henry B. Fahnbulleh; People's Democratic Party of Liberia (PDPL)—George T. Washington; United People's Party (UPP)—Gabriel B. Matthews; National Democratic Party of Liberia (NDPL)—George E. S. Boley Sr.; and Liberia People's Party (LPP)—Togba Nah Tipoteh.

With a high voter turnout—90 percent of some one million registered voters—the elections were adjudged free and fair in the circumstances. The NPFL's Charles Taylor won an overwhelming victory in the presidential elections, as the people wisely opted to validate his military victory at the polls to avert a continuation of the war, and his party took 75 percent of the Senate and House of Representatives seats by proportional representation. The Taylor government was inaugurated on August 2, 1997, with a semblance of popular support and legitimacy, and the shooting war finally ended. However, the country's infrastructure lay in ruins, and thousands of people became refugees in Liberia and foreign countries. Worse still, Taylor's involvement in the festering and brutal civil war in neighboring Sierra Leone, where his allies committed bestial atrocities, cast a dark shadow on his government. Indeed, his government never lived down the negative image it acquired from its involvement in the "blood diamonds" saga in Sierra Leone (where rebels mined and exported diamonds and used the proceeds to buy weapons; the illicit traffic enriched warloards, who used forced labor in the mines).

In any case, in spite of loud proclamations, Taylor's government did not achieve much socioeconomic transformation of the country, in part because of the unwillingness of international donors to commit themselves fully to the task of reconstruction. This was largely because of the aforementioned image problem, which was not helped by the government's record of human rights abuses, including murders, and the arbitrary exercise of power. Unemployment and underemployment remained high. To be fair, the Taylor government ensured the territorial integrity of the country, and the country enjoyed a semblance of peace and stability up to 1999. But it failed to attract the expected magnitude of investor and donor support that was sorely needed in the reconstruction of a war-ravaged country. Paradoxically, Taylor and his cronies, like many of their counterparts in the region, diverted much of the foreign aid into their private accounts. From 1999 to 2003, the Taylor government came under increasing domestic and international pressure as Nigeria and Ghana, two important regional powers, accused the Taylor government of continuing involvement in the Sierra Leonian tragedy. Liberia was accordingly sanctioned by and isolated from the international community. The climax came on June 2, 2003, when a UN tribunal formally indicted Taylor on charges of war crimes in Sierra Leone.

Meanwhile, at home, discontent gradually degenerated into armed opposition with the emergence of two major liberation movements—the Movement for Democracy in Liberia (MODEL), supported mainly by the Khran kins of Samuel Doe, and Liberians United for Reconciliation and Democracy (LURD), which was apparently funded and supported by the neighboring state of Guinea. The military successes of the two movements between 2000 and 2003, akin to those of the NPFL in the previous decade, generated another round of war-induced misery, displacement of persons, and considerable destruction of life and property. Again, it took the intervention of regional powers to broker peace between the Taylor government and the insurgents, who had advanced as far as the capital city of Monrovia. By a peace agreement signed in Accra, Ghana, in June 2003, Taylor agreed to step down as president and go into exile as part of a solution to the crisis. Although he reneged on the agreement, he was finally forced into exile in Nigeria on August 11, 2003, as LURD forces put pressure on Monrovia, the government having lost control of two-thirds of the country to LURD and MODEL forces.

It then fell to Taylor's vice president and interim president, Moses Blah, to reach a final accord with the insurgents. With security provided by 3,600 peace-keeping troops of the ECOWAS Mission to Liberia (ECOMIL), backed by American financial and logistic support, the factions signed a comprehensive peace agreement. A national government with a two-year tenure was selected on August 21, 2003. Gyude Bryant and Wesley Johnson were appointed chair and vice chair, respectively, of the National Transitional Government of Liberia (NTGL), which was to hold fort till January 2006, when it would be replaced by winners of elections to be held in October 2005. The transitional government was made up of 12 representatives each of LURD, MODEL, and the existing government in a 76-member legislative assembly. The government embarked on the disarmament program; by April 2004 it had succeeded in disarming half the combatants, and by June it had commenced the process of their reintegration into society. Still, the UN maintained its embargo of Liberian timber and diamond exports pending the full return to peace. Meanwhile, the NTGL too has faced allegations of corruption and has not been able to establish its authority over parts of the country.

NOTES

1. D. Elwood Dunn, Amos J. Beyan, and Carl Patrick Burrowes, *Historical Dictionary of Liberia,* 2nd ed. (Metuchen, N.J.: Scarecrow Press, 2001).
2. Ibid.

REFERENCES

Dunn, D. Elwood, Amos J. Bevan, and Carl Patrick Burrowes. *Historical Dictionary of Liberia,* 2nd ed. Metuchen, N.J.: Scarecrow Press, 2001.

Levy, Patricia. *Liberia,* 2nd ed. New York: Benchmark Books, 1998.

Liebenow, J. G. *Liberia: The Quest for Democracy.* Bloomington: Indiana University Press, 1987.

Osaghae, Eghosa E. *Ethnicity, Class and the Struggle for State Power in Liberia.* Dakar, Senegal: CODESRIA, 1996.

Saha, Santosh C. *Culture in Liberia: An Afrocentric View of the Cultural Intercation between the Indigenous Liberians and the Americo-Liberians.* Lewiston, N.Y.: Edwin Mellen Press, 1998.

2

Religion and Worldview

Belief that all power has its origin in the invisible world, where God and spirits
dwell, is a constant of Liberian history.
— Stephen Ellis, anthropologist and historian[1]

THIS CHAPTER ANALYZES the dimensions of the religious beliefs and worldview
of Liberian peoples across space and time. Indigenous beliefs and worldview,
and the impact on them of Islam and Christianity and their accompanying
worldviews, are considered along with the interactions of religion with politics, medicine, and business. This exercise provides insights into the indigenous religious beliefs and worldview of Liberians, the alternatives offered by
Islam and Christianity, and the interactions of these elements. Indeed, accommodation in religious practice has been the dominant trend among Liberians.
The widespread tendency to combine diverse beliefs is attributable to the
opportunistic strategy of hedging one's bets by exploring multiple options to
procure solutions to a broad range of problems.

The moral dilemma faced when the demands of the different religions
become irreconcilable is eventually resolved on the altar of expediency. Hence,
it is possible to generalize that in spite of their differences in religious convictions and outlook, most Liberians assign a leading, if not fundamental,
importance to spiritual forces and powers in their daily lives and fortunes.
Virtually everyone believes in life after death, a reality that is buttressed by the
veneration of ancestors, at whose graves prayers and sacrifices are offered.
This practice is based on the conviction that ancestors would intercede on
behalf of their offspring to avert disaster or to achieve some positive end.

Most Liberians are also agreed that propitiation involving sacrifice is required to negotiate human relationships with the supernatural world.

Until the advent of Islam and Christianity, the religious beliefs and world-views of Liberians were shaped by birth and residence. That is, everyone was born into the prevailing system in their clan or village, and the emphasis was on harmony among the living members on the one hand, and between living members and ancestors on the other. Indigenous societies were not compart-mentalized into religious spheres and nonreligious spheres (such as politics). Life was treated as a whole, comprising different but complementary parts.

Yet it must be acknowledged that the Liberian civil war has had a pro-found impact on people's beliefs and worldview. Indigenous religion was severely affected by certain acts committed during the war that amounted to desecration. For example, sacred forests and shrines were violated by hostile combatants—such as the Muslim Mandingo militia—while masks that had been deemed sacred were exposed to the glare of noninitiates, including women. The atrocities and sacrilegious acts committed during the war pro-foundly assaulted the psyche of ordinary Liberians and outraged the priests and defenders of the traditional order. Christian ministers, especially the Pentecostals, have been active in the aftermath of the war to ameliorate through their preaching and charitable work the emotional, psychological, and material damage done by the war.

TRADITIONAL OR INDIGENOUS RELIGION AND WORLDVIEW

Given the nature of its evolution, specifically, the dominance of America-Liberians in the formation of the country, there is a general impression that Liberia is a Christian state. Indeed, emigrants from the United States and the Caribbean were steeped in the dominant Western/Christian worldview in their countries of departure. But this perception is misleading because the settlers also brought the Western practice of freemasonry with them. Indeed, freemasonry was one of the pillars of the True Whig Party, the party that dominated government and public life in pre-1980 Liberia. Moreover, if the settlements established along the coast by the America-Liberians were domi-nated by Christians, the same could not be said of the hinterland communi-ties, where more than 95 percent of the people of Liberia lived.

There, indigenous religious beliefs held sway together with Islam, a religion associated with the Mandingo, Vai, Gola, and Gbandi of western Liberia. These parts of the hinterland were also proximate to Sierra Leone and Guinea, where there were considerable Muslim populations. A 2002 estimate put the religious affiliations of Liberians at 40 percent Traditionalists, 40 percent Christians, and 20 percent Muslims. As will be shown in this chapter, in many cases there are no sharp lines of demarcation along religious lines in that many Liberians, like their counterparts in other places in West Africa, owed concurrent allegiance to multiple faiths.

Hence, in examining the religion and worldview of Liberians, the multiplicity of belief and thought systems has to be accepted as fundamental to an understanding of the discussion in this chapter. A second general remark is that, regardless of the religious affiliation of Liberians, they all share a common outlook on the supernatural and the keeping of secrets. Liberian religious culture broadly defined is characterized by a predisposition toward secrecy (encapsulated in the concept of *ifa mo*—"do not speak it") and an ingrained belief in the intervention of mysterious forces in human affairs. Regardless—or because—of their religious preferences, Liberians acknowledge the power of evil in human affairs.

For instance, President William R. Tolbert (1971–80) had a phobia about sleeping in the Executive Mansion, as the president's official residence is called, and instead commuted to work from his own residence some twenty-five miles outside the capital. Ironically, it was on the night he did sleep in the executive mansion that he was assassinated (April 12, 1980). It was reported that Tolbert had been put off by evidence of ritual practices in the mansion carried out by his predecessor, William V. S. Tubman (1944–71), another irony given that Tolbert was a church minister in his own right and Tubman, though openly identifying with freemasonry, was also a Christian by popular definition. The point is that both elite and nonelite Liberians usually attribute events to the activities of secret powers and forces.

This explains why President Samuel Doe (1980–90) was widely believed to be endowed with great supernatural powers (an idea that he himself popularized in a famous boast that the gun that could kill him had not been manufactured) even by those who captured him and later tortured him to death. Doe's ghastly death was also given spiritual interpretations rather than being attributed to tactical miscalculation or sheer coincidence. Indeed, a female supporter of Doe was said to have dreamt on the night before his abduction and execution that she saw him being carried off by angels, a dream that was later understood to represent a clear premonition of his impending demise. It is worth stating in passing that belief in dreams as a medium of conveying messages from the spirit world is an essential part of religious convictions and worldview in Liberia, as in other parts of Africa.

Moreover, the fundamental belief of Liberians in the supernatural is illustrated by the fact that Doe, like a good number of his compatriots of all religious persuasions, fortified himself with various charms in open and intimate parts of the body, which were discovered (and presumably appropriated) by his captors. The brutality with which he was handled derived as much from vengeance as from the strong conviction that he had potent charms that could make him disappear at will if given some breathing space. The point is that, regardless of their advertised claims to affiliation with Christianity, the two ill-fated Liberian presidents—Tolbert and Doe—were still attached to the beliefs held by a vast majority of their countrymen and countrywomen. Such beliefs include the conviction that there are deep and hidden things about an individual that only diviners, priests, and other qualified persons can unravel. This presupposes that whatever exists or happens in the physical realm has foundations in the spirit world. Among the Gio, the force behind every creature is known as *du,* everyone being a manifestation of their own *du.*

Belief in spirits has always been fundamental to Liberian life, worldview, and religious beliefs. Traditional religionists, especially those in the Poro areas of northern and northwestern Liberia, believe in the existence of a variety of spirits: ancestral spirits, various water and bush spirits, genies, spirits of the associations, and specific Poro spirits. Ancestral spirits are believed to protect and play mediatory roles in the affairs of their offspring and in their offspring's dealings with the spirit world, and generally maintain an interest in their well-being. Bush and water spirits and genies are believed to possess humans and to be capable of transferring specialized knowledge or power to them. This consequently has led to the emergence of specialized priests, diviners, physicians, and fortune-tellers who themselves claim to communicate with the spirits. These spirits are also believed to govern the mysterious world that exists outside of human control. Spirits (or totems) of the associations govern the affairs of the snake and leopard societies, which often act as the agents of the Poro. The Poro spirits include the bush devil, which communicates the will of the god and acts as its earthly or visible manifestations. These spirits are represented by several masked dancers under the control of the Poro.

The spirit world of benign and malevolent spirits and ancestors is usually represented by masquerades in which participants wear wooden masks. Though the man behind the mask is a mere mortal, the wooden mask shields his identity from the human gaze, and the ancestral spirit or any spiritual force that comes upon him is believed to take him beyond the level of non-initiates. In that case, it makes sense to keep secrets and mask intentions in a society living in awe of the unseen, supernatural world. A striking example of the attribution of potent spiritual power to tangible objects is the popular perception of the Statue of the Unknown Soldier, erected in Monrovia after the April 1980 coup, as an object endowed with such powers. These alleged powers did not, however, save the statue from destruction by artillery fire during heavy fighting for control of Monrovia in April 1996. In essence, it is commonly held that the unseen gods and spirits represent the ultimate source of power, and humans have to arrange how to communicate with or appease such spiritual forces. Yet it is important to concede not only that these beliefs vary in their details but also that they are more grounded in some parts of the country than others. Thus, given the antiquity of the Poro and Sande (male and female societies, respectively) in the central regions, they are more intricately woven into the fabric of society and politics in those places than in southeastern Liberia.

Whether considered in terms of their political and social functions, or more narrowly as religious fraternities, Poro and Sande encapsulate the religious and general worldviews of most Liberian peoples. Poro is well established among the Gola, the Vai, and many of the Mandingos of western Liberia, the Mende, Loma, Gbandi, Kissi, and Belle to the northwest and the Kpelle and elements of the Mano and Bassa of the central region. It has close ties with the earth and forest, and this explains why noninitiates, especially so-called civilized Liberians (presumably Christians or Americo-Liberians) of Monrovia and other places associate it with the bush devil. Such a characterization is pejorative in that it attributes evil to Poro and Sande, and to all who are associated with them because of their esoteric or secret practices. As might be expected, the bush or forest is associated with mystery, hiding, and danger since it is the dwelling of dangerous animals and, presumably, malevolent spirits. Though more deeply entrenched in the northwest region of Liberia, Poro and Sande do exist in other parts of the country. Still, the Kruan people of southeastern Liberia are not known to have had the Poro and Sande, though they have their own secret societies that serve similar religious and other functions.

These societies, especially Poro, exist in the various communities under the control of local councils of elders. All adult males and females in the community belonged to Poro and Sande, which means that the societies are not as secret as often claimed. But it is true that their teachings and beliefs are the preserve of the initiates and are thus secret to the extent that the societies transmit esoteric knowledge and impart specialized skills in the management of societal problems, such as medical skills in treating snakebites. Even within the Poro, for example, lower-cadre initiatives are ignorant of knowledge reserved to higher-level members or leaders.

One of the social functions of societies like Poro and Sande is to deter antisocial behavior or beliefs. Hence, the detection or suppression of witchcraft was carried out by the kui societies among the Grebo of southeastern Liberia as late as the early twentieth century. This entailed the killing of convicts as a means of ridding the society of evil. In the Poro areas, such as among the Kpelle, cases of supposed witchcraft were determined by the Poro elders within their conclave.

Another traditional religious practice that is common in parts of Liberia is totemism, in which particular animals are venerated as possessing spiritual powers. Such animals include crocodiles or leopards. During the initial stages of the NPFL offensive from Nimba County in 1989–90, a marauding human-eating leopard was reported to be on the prowl; this was understood to have spiritual implications, hinging on the traditional belief that spirits (whether of an animal, the forest, or a dead ancestor) could possess human beings. Animals too are believed to be possessed.

It is important to clarify the point that the prowling leopard might well have been a human who was supposedly possessed by the spirit of the leopard and went about killing with a special knife that left wound marks that appeared as though they had been inflicted by the claws of a leopard. Spirit possession is also believed to be possible through masks, the use of which symbolizes connection with the invisible forces in the spirit world. Thus, according to the Gio, one person's *du*, which exists independent of him or her, can move into or possess another person. For many Liberians, the spirit world enables two-way traffic: humans can enter it, and spirits also enter (possess) humans. Thus, people are transformed into spirits in their sleep; they can also be transformed into animals when they are possessed by the spirit of particular animals, such as leopards; and a person can be possessed by the spirit of another human being or a devil.

A vital aspect of traditional Liberian religion and worldview concerns the continuity of the human spirit beyond death. This is given expression in various ways. First is the belief in the return of ancestral spirits through masquerades. Prayers are therefore offered to ancestors. Second is the practice, which became rife during the Liberian civil war, of eating the heart (or other body parts) of a dead human, especially a great or brave person, in the hope of either ensuring the continuity of that person's spirit or appropriating that person's spiritual potency by inheritance or appropriation. Such was the fate of initiates who died during their seclusion in the Poro bush school (a camp in the forest where initiates were groomed) and who were deemed to have been eaten by the bush devil.

Human sacrifice in premodern times too was an ancient manifestation of this belief in the continuity of the human spirit. It was often required when a *zoe* (a priest of Poro) aspired to a higher office in the Poro, and such persons might have had to offer their own sons in sacrifice. Such an act was acknowledged, as in the Christian doctrine of the crucifixion of Christ, as the ultimate and most potent sacrifice. But instances of such human sacrifice were certainly few and far between in those days, and the practice is a rarity today, though there are rumors of its persistence.

Whatever the differences across regions, counties, and ethnic groups, indigenous religion and worldview differ from those of world religions such as Christianity and Islam. First, there exist a multiplicity of deities and spirits, unlike the monotheism of the world religions. Though the indigenous peoples believe in the existence of a supreme being (Great Spirit), they also recognize the existence of lesser gods and spirits that bear a variety of names given by the various ethnic groups in the country. The lesser spirits are understood to be of two types: those that were created as spirits and had never assumed a human identity, and humans who were deified after their death. Second, the sharp distinction between good (God) and evil (Satan) is not represented in indigenous religion and worldview, though such notions are increasingly becoming dominant in a society that has come under the increasing influence of Christianity and Islam.

Hence, the supreme being among the Vai (called Kamba), which coexists with lesser spirits called *dudane,* is acknowledged as the Creator, who is the fountain of both good and evil. In the worldview represented by Poro theology, for example, there is a certain ambivalence in that the spirit of the forest is believed to be both malevolent and benevolent, depending on the circumstances. Hence, it is understood that Poro priests (*zoes*) could sacrifice their own close relations to attain a higher level of spiritual power, and can also execute social deviants. Both cases of human sacrifice, abhorrent as they may seem today, were in the past accepted as unavoidable in the quest to maintain the integrity of the social order, and these sacrifices were not seen as evil if they were carried out for the aforementioned reasons and seemingly for the ultimate good of the larger community.

A third general feature of indigenous religious belief and worldview is the propitiation of ancestral and other spirits, particularly after a misfortune has befallen an individual or the community on account of the presumed misdeeds of the victims. Divination is usually carried out to determine the cause of such occurrences as well as the appropriate propitiatory rites, often involving (animal) sacrifice. Fourth, ancestors are venerated and prayers made through them to the higher spiritual authorities or supreme being (called *yala* by the Kpelle). Ancestors are considered to be the most efficacious intercessors in that the ancestor spirits know best how to make the supplication that elicits the best possible solutions or answers. Fifth, African indigenous religions do not have founders, prophets, or holy books like Christianity and Islam. Still, the tenets of religious observances have been preserved through rituals, myths, songs, parables, and various traditions passed down through the generations. Also unlike the aforementioned universal religions, the indigenous religions of Liberia were not propagated by missionaries or a specialized class of functionaries. However, religious institutions like the Poro and Sande spread across the Liberian hinterland through conquest and assimilation.

CHRISTIANITY IN LIBERIA

Christianity was introduced into Liberia with the settlement of the Americo-Liberians in the 1820s. Various Christian missions, including Baptists, Presbyterians, Episcopalians, and Congregationalists, accordingly established their stations in the coastal regions. The dominant Christian denomination in Liberia has been the Liberian Methodist Church, which was planted with the arrival of the first Americo-Liberian settlers on January 7, 1822. Prominent Liberian leaders, such as presidents J. J. Roberts and William V. S. Tubman, were Methodists. Until 1964, the Liberian Methodist Church was supervised by U.S. missionaries and, later, a missionary bishop in South Africa. In 1944, the supervision of the Liberian Church was vested in the Central Jurisdiction in the United States, which authorized the election of a bishop dedicated solely to serving Liberia. Finally, in 1964, Liberia's first bishop of the Methodist Church, Stephen Trowen Nagbe, was elected. At his death in 1972, he was succeeded by another indigenous Liberian, Bennie D. Warner, who in 1977 became Liberia's vice president under President Tolbert, a clear marriage of church and state, especially given that Tolbert was a Baptist minister in his own right.

Although the Methodists initially focused on the Americo-Liberians, they soon joined other Christian missions in launching into the Liberian hinterland. They were preceded in this endeavor by the Protestant Episcopal Church, which pioneered the evangelization of the Grebo. The Methodists too established schools and churches in the Cape Palmas region.

The Lutheran Church of America began its first African mission in Liberia in 1860 when it founded the Liberian Lutheran Mission. The Lutheran Mission's uniqueness was further reinforced by its decision to venture into the hinterland, a departure from the tradition of older Missions that remained along the coast. Hence, it concentrated its efforts on the Loma and Kpelle of central and northwestern Liberia. Accordingly, its first Liberian bishop, Roland J. Payne, earned the sobriquet "the Jungle Bishop" on account of the rural focus of the church. The mission introduced formal education and pursued a literacy program to serve the rural communities where it operated. It emphasized evangelization and literacy in the indigenous languages and later provided translations of the Bible into Loma and Kpelle so that the people could worship God in their own languages. The mission undertook a transition in leadership from American missionaries to indigenous clergy that was accomplished in 1965 when the first indigenous bishop was appointed. The Lutheran church also made a mark in its ecumenical endeavors by cooperating with the Episcopal church in the running of a hospital at Suakoko and with other churches to operate a radio and television station, a school of theology, and a Sunday school curriculum project.

Methodist Church, Monrovia. Courtesy of the Library of Congress.

The pioneer missions were joined during the twentieth century by newer denominations including Roman Catholic, Seventh-Day Adventist, Pentecostal (such as Assemblies of God, the Pentecostal Assembly of the World, and the Pentecostal Assembly of Canada) and African churches, such as the Aladura (meaning "those who pray") churches from the West African country of Nigeria, hundreds of miles to the east. A notable presence in Liberia was the Sudan Interior Mission, which operated Radio ELWA (Eternal Love Winning Africa), the impact of which extended far beyond the borders of Liberia. The doctrines of these churches are expectedly diverse, but they have all come to accommodate aspects of indigenous beliefs as outlined previously.

In effect, many Liberian Christians, like their counterparts elsewhere in West Africa except the Pentecostals, think nothing of concurrent adherence to diverse religious beliefs. In this sense, Liberia conforms to a general pattern in Africa where practices associated with indigenous religion—such as spirit possession and soothsaying—have been appropriated into Christian liturgy. The Aladura and other spiritual churches emphasize prophecy (which tallies with divination in indigenous religion), the use of tangible objects like holy water in a bottle, and the casting out of demons. Some of these Christians also offer animal sacrifice if required by any diviner.

As a general observation, independent churches like the Aladura are distinguished not only by their emphasis on baptism, dreams, and prophecies, but also by the class of their membership. By and large, their members are drawn from the lower classes, for whom their liturgy provides a form of self-expression.

Worship in such churches involves singing, clapping, drumming, dancing, and a lack of restraint that is alien to the mainstream missions. It is commonly assumed that such modes of worship permit church members to let off steam and obtain relief from their frustrations in life. The members also derive security and personal advancement in the church hierarchy from their membership.

Since the era of Americo-Liberian rule, and especially from the 1930s, supposedly Christian Americo-Liberian political and business elite have combined the profession of Christianity with freemasonry and indigenous beliefs. President D. B. King (1920–30) was the first Liberian head of state to be associated with the Poro and was alleged to have joined the Alligator Society. One of his successors, William V. S. Tubman, was reputed to have been the head of all the Poro societies in the country, and his wife too was initiated into the Sande. This was additional to Tubman's official classification as a Christian (Methodist) and a freemason. Even Tolbert, an acclaimed Baptist minister, indeed, the president of the World Baptist Alliance, was also a *zo*.

The Liberian civil war of the 1980s and 1990s did not spare the church in that combatants freely desecrated shrines and pillaged churches and mosques. Allusion has been made to the desecration of Poro shrines and sacred groves, but possibly the worst atrocity was the massacre in July 1990 of 600 persons who had sought refuge in St. Peter's Lutheran church in Liberia, an outrage attributed to the soldiers of President Samuel K. Doe. Throughout the war, churches were looted and structures such as churches. school buildings, and hospitals were vandalized by combatants of the various armed militias. Ministers and their congregations were forced to flee for their lives, the survivors becoming destitute refugees and internally displaced persons.

The rise of Pentecostal Christianity, especially since the Liberian civil war, has challenged the dominant trend of Christianity that has come to terms with non-Christian beliefs. The central thrust of Pentecostal denominations is the preaching of the born-again experience, with the promise of a new life following confession of sins and the renunciation of past sinful deeds. Pentecostal churches also share adherence to the doctrine of believers' personal experience of Holy Spirit baptism, as was the case at Pentecost in the early church. Although an increasing number of Pentecostals are now better educated and well placed in society, the early converts tended to be persons of more humble pedigree.

The Pentecostal phenomenon has been given a fillip by the trauma of the Liberian civil war. Although the central idea of being born again is about spiritual rebirth, it has had a therapeutic impact on a society in which thousands of citizens were brutalized directly as victims or perpetrators of war crimes and atrocities. The stark reality of the evil represented by the killings, population displacements, rape, and ritual murder has given Pentecostal preachers abundant fodder for their sermons. Consequently, in the aftermath of the war, many former combatants, including child soldiers, have proclaimed a newfound faith in the redemption offered by the Pentecostal ministries that sprouted in Monrovia and other notable settlements. The Pentecostals have argued that the war was the work of the Satan and was a divine punishment for the sins of the people. They attributed God's displeasure to the people's attachment to traditional religions and the perpetration of ritual murder.

An additional development in the Christian community since the civil war has been the upsurge in churches emphasizing healing, miracles, and prosperity in their teachings. Such churches could also be seen as contributing to the healing process in the country by promising relief from physical ailments and material destitution, and by claiming power over so-called evil powers or agents of Satan. They attract large crowds not only because they proffer solutions to problems of daily existence, but also because their message and methods resonate with the people. Liberians are quite familiar with the techniques and vocabulary employed by the preachers, which are akin to those used by traditional priests and diviners. However, orthodox Pentecostal Christians are generally critical of this trend because they suspect that many of the healing- or prosperity-oriented Pentecostal ministries are fake and that their leaders employ evil powers and oratory to deceive the unwary.

In all, the advent of Christianity has affected the religious structure and worldview of Liberian communities in several ways. First, it has contributed to the diversity of the religious beliefs of Liberian peoples. Second, Christianity has been the harbinger of Western education and literacy through its establishment of mission schools. Such schools produced the first crop of the Western-educated elite in the indigenous societies of the Liberian hinterland. Third, the Christian missions also pioneered the application of Western medicine to many of the diseases and plagues that had ravaged many of these communities. Though the facilities provided by the missions were rudimentary, they did lay the foundation for later efforts by the government. Fourth, the aggressive evangelization of many of the indigenous Liberian communities was attended by the wholesale condemnation of many indigenous practices as pagan or barbaric, leading to the erosion of the social fabric of the community and the loss of several cultural artifacts. However, the rise of independent African churches has meant the infusion of aspects of indigenous culture and tradition into the beliefs and liturgy of the Christian churches. Drums and indigenous music have been incorporated into Christian worship, as have some indigenous rituals.

Islam in Liberia

Although Islam was a dominant religion in medieval western Sudan, covering the savannah region to the north of the Liberian forests, historical accounts indicate that the ancient Mali empire was the first Sahelian empire (the Sahel is the zone between the Guinea forest and the Sahara desert) to extend its reach to the forest fringes. However, the forest dwellers who were subjects of the Mali rulers did not embrace Islam, and only in the early nineteenth century did the religion make headway with the coming of the Mandingo. Reputed to be descendants of the Muslim ruling dynasty of Mali, the Mandingo (offshoots of the Malinke branch of the Mande-speaking peoples) moved into the territory of modern Liberia primarily as traders who also proselytized. Mandingo traders consciously propagated Islam as they conducted their business and came to dominate the long-distance trade of the Liberian hinterland. Their business acumen aided their proselytization as their commercial success attracted converts to Islam. The informal efforts of the traders were complemented and reinforced by those of Muslim clerics (known variously as *karamokos,* marabouts, and *mori,* among other names), who established Quranic schools and mosques, purveyed charms and amulets, and offered spiritual guidance to some local rulers. Commercial expansion aided the spread of Islam in that the religion served as a bond among traders in a widening network of regional trade.

The spread of Islam in the Liberian hinterland was thus facilitated by a combination of factors: the commercial activities of the Mandingo (or Dyula) traders, the establishment of Islamic educational institutions, and intermarriage with non-Muslims.. During the nineteenth century, Islam increasingly became the religion of trade in many parts of the West African Sahel and the adjoining parts of the forest region. Consequently, conversion to Islam was seen by many aspiring indigenous traders as a way of getting into the network of regional trade dominated by Muslims. The new convert anticipated, and often got, financial and moral support from his coreligionists.

Islam also spread through the educational services and facilities that it offered to the peoples of a preliterate society. With an initial focus on local notables in the various communities, the Mandingo and other Muslim elements soon ingratiated themselves with the indigenous peoples. Sons of local notables passed through the Quranic schools, where they learned Arabic and were inducted into the Islamic faith. Graduates of such schools put their literacy to use by communicating in their indigenous languages. The Kpelle and Vai, two of Liberia's indigenous peoples, soon acquired a reputation for writing their own languages in the Islamic script. Islamic literacy facilitated trade and the writing of commercial contracts. Islam also spread through the activities of

Muslim diviners, whose trade found a ready clientele in a community in which divination was a pillar of indigenous religion. The increasingly widespread reputation of the potency of charms or amulets prepared by Muslim clerics also boosted the numbers of their clientele. Muslim diviners were employed to make powerful charms to ward off malevolent spirits or offer prayers or sacrifice for chiefs going to war or communities seeking divine favor.

The practice of Muslim men marrying non-Muslim women also aided the spread of Islam. The Mandingo, for example, usually did this without allowing their own women to marry non-Muslim men; they reasoned that children were likely to adopt the faith of their fathers. Hence, the ranks of Muslims would swell through intermarriage if Muslim men married non-Muslim women rather than the reverse. In this way, Muslim men were actively involved in the propagation of Islam in that their non-Muslim wives tended to convert in due course. In addition, Islam found a willing audience among the indigenous African peoples of Liberia because, unlike Christianity, it was more tolerant of indigenous cultural practices, such as polygyny. Islam also did not condemn slavery, the ancient practice of divination, veneration of ancestors, or propitiation through sacrifice.

Islam spread slowly by the foregoing means in the Liberian hinterland. The Vai and Loma were the earliest indigenous people to convert to Islam. The Vai had had commercial relations with the Mandingo, with whom they shared cultural and linguistic ties that predisposed them to accepting the new religion propagated by the latter. This took place in the early nineteenth century. Vai chiefs welcomed Mandingo Muslim clerics who were soon engaged as advisers. The latter were rewarded with wives and secured land for their settlement.

The Vai were heavily Islamized in the twentieth century because of certain developments associated with the incursion of the central government from Monrovia. First, the utter failure of the traditional authorities and ancestral spirits to ward off the America-Liberian government invasion created deep doubts in the efficacy of the indigenous political and religious authorities, such as the Poro. Second, when the Liberian government had established its authority in the Vai territory by the 1920s, its decision to rid the Poro of the traditional power to inflict capital punishment further eroded the basis of the latter's authority. Third, the Liberian government also abolished internal servitude and thereby caused a social revolution in Vai society when the servile classes left for urban areas or their homelands. This development further alienated the Vai from the Monrovia government and its influence, including Christianity, and made Islam a more attractive alternative. Fourth, the Vai elite were skeptical about Christianity because the America-Liberians, who propagated it, were perceived as unfit (as former slaves) to train their own children, who were born free.

The gap created by these developments was filled by Islam, which had existed all along as an alternative (or a complement) to the indigenous religious and social systems. Hence, by the mid-twentieth century, Vai society had become heavily saturated with Islamic influence. It was easy for the Vai to identify with the Muslim supreme being (Allah) given their traditional understanding or conception of Kangmba (or Kamba) as the supreme being. Consequently, they generally abandoned the traditional funeral practices, among others, for the Islamic and withdrew their patronage of Poro, which virtually disappeared from their land. Where Poro survived, the length of time spent in the bush schools was reduced from four years to a couple of days.

Yet many of the converts to Islam in the Liberian hinterland still retained much of their traditional religious beliefs and practices. It has been suggested that the spread of Islam followed the trail of Mandingo commercial activities and settlement in the Liberian hinterland. Hence, other Liberian peoples, notably the Bassa, Kpelle, Mano, and Gio, converted to Islam as the Mandingo moved into their territories, and this explains why the leading commercial centers in those places (such as Ganta, Gbarnga, Saniquellie, and Voinjama) contain large numbers of Muslims.

Consequently, Islam, though a religion of the minority, has exerted considerable influence on the culture and customs of Liberian peoples. First, it has had some impact on the educational system of the indigenous societies through the secular, moral, and spiritual instructions disseminated through Quranic schools and mosques. The literacy that accompanies Islamic proselytization has aided the development of literacy in local languages and the development of indigenous scripts. Second, Islam has affected traditional practices such as marriage, child naming, burial, and business. Islamic or Arabic names have now been adopted by individuals and families, while business transactions have been guided by the prescriptions of the religion. Popular Islamic names that have been adopted by Liberian Muslims include Bockari (Abu Bakr), Momodu (Muhammad), and Brimah (Ibrahim); this practice also exemplifies how these names (and Islam, too) have been indigenized in the peoples' local languages.

Third, Islam has created a distinct identity and shared values for its votaries. Islamic religious practices and observances such as the mandatory fast, annual calendar of feasts, and call to prayers have permeated the fabric of many communities across the country. More telling is the way Islam has reached an accommodation with the indigenous systems of thought and belief almost to the point of subverting them. Muslim spiritualists, known as *moriman,* make charms from passages of the Quran, the ascribed potency of which has rivaled, if not supplanted, that attributed to the indigenous ones.

In the same vein, Islamic practices have influenced as well as incorporated Vai religious observances. Fourth, Islam has provided a vehicle for intergroup relations in the Liberian hinterland. It has facilitated the integration of the Mandingo settlers into the indigenous society and even ensured the infiltration of Mandingo words into the languages of the Gola, Kpelle, and Vai. This has also been extended to the adoption of Mandingo names—such as Kroma (Koroma), Kamara, Sirleaf (Sheriff), and Turay—by clans and lineages in the indigenous ethnic groups of the hinterland.

Fifth, Islam has altered the lifestyle of the indigenous peoples who embraced it. Many of the male converts abstained from drinking alcoholic beverages and from eating pork, monkeys, and animals that had not been slaughtered in the prescribed manner. Converts have had to conform to the peculiar observances of Islam—the mandatory daily five prayers, the Ramadan fast, the giving of alms, and the hajj (pilgrimage to Mecca). As indicated in Chapter 7, the funeral practices of Liberian Muslims necessarily follow Islamic injunctions. In the same vein, Islamic flowing dress has been adopted by converts.

That said, Islam did not march unchallenged through the Liberian hinterland. It ran into stiff resistance in the territory of the Gbandi of Lofa County, where the relatively highly centralized social and political systems, underpinned by a resilient culture, provided a bulwark against the Mandingo purveyors of Islam. This resulted in the negligibility of the Islamic impact on Gbandi society, in contrast to the warm reception among the Vai, for example, and accommodation by the Kpelle. The latter adopted a number of Islamic institutions but retained the traditional basis of their culture. If the opposition of the Gbandi can be attributed to their traditional culture, that of the Americo-Liberians derived from the traditional cleavage between Christianity and Islam. More than that, the Americo-Liberian government in Monrovia also saw a potential threat to its ascendancy and to the spread of Western education in the expansion of Islam and Quranic education. Hence, it supported the expansion of Christian missions into the hinterland as a counterweight to the perceived threat.

A striking feature of Liberian Islam is that its adherents are orthodox Sunni, though there are Shia Muslims among the Lebanese settlers in the country.[2] In addition, from the mid-1950s, the Ahmadiya, a sect that is considered heretical by other Muslims, has been established in Liberia, but its impact has been minimal. In all, in spite of the hostility of the Americo-Liberian government and the Christian missionaries, Islam has held its own among Liberian peoples such as the Mandingo and Vai, 90 and 75 percent of whom, respectively, are Muslims.

OTHER RELIGIOUS MOVEMENTS

In spite of the dominance of Christianity from the founding of Liberia in the nineteenth century and the presence of Islam as the religion of some indigenous peoples, other faiths have won adherents among Liberians. A major quasi-religious ideology is freemasonry, which was introduced with the settlement of the Americo-Liberians. The Masonic Order was established in 1851 and counted among its votaries leading personalities in the Liberian establishment. At least five presidents of Liberia, beginning with J. J. Roberts, became grand masters of the Order. Although these leading members were officially classified as Christians, they were committed to freemasonry because it embodied the ideals of the community and symbolized the solidarity of the Americo-Liberians. The Masonic conclaves provided a rather secretive ambience for discussing and reaching a consensus on important affairs of the country before they were thrown open for general discussion in public places like the parliament. The Masonic lodges also gave their members an unassailable advantage over noninitiates in the quest for jobs, business, political appointments, and even justice.

The emergence in 1970 of the Kingdom Assembly Church of Africa, founded by Richard K. Sleboe, an indigene of Sinoe County, was a unique event in the religious history of Liberia. Sleboe, a former adherent of the Jehovah's Witness movement, preached the doctrine of physical immortality, which assured his followers of freedom from death. His religious group came to be known as the "never-die church," though mainstream Christian missions regarded its doctrine as heretical. Whereas mainstream Christians believed in the immortality of the human soul after physical death and its transport to another realm known as heaven, Sleboe and his followers held that they would not die but would live on and inherit the earth, a carryover from the teachings of the Jehovah's Witnesses. More controversial was Sleboe's claim to divinity, which nevertheless did not rob him of support among his adherents. He assumed the title of "Counsellor" and "Prince of Peace," appellations of the Holy Spirit and Jesus, respectively. However, his death in 1986 dealt a fatal blow to his reputation, and this led to mass withdrawal from his movement. Some die-hards remained nonetheless, but they split into two groups with different explanations for the debacle caused by their founder's death. It is significant that members of the groups chose to ignore the evidence contradicting their core beliefs: Sleboe's death ordinarily cast doubt on his divinity, while his death and the demise of members' relations belied the claim of immortality. The resilience of the so-called never-die doctrine is bewildering in the face of the crises of the post-1980 years.

RELIGION AND POLITICS

The three dominant religious systems in Liberia have not been immune from politics; conversely, they either have been inseparable from it or have been employed as a tool of political struggles. The Poro and Sande (and their counterparts among the Kruan peoples of southeastern Liberia) as the central religious institutions of many of the country's indigenous peoples represented the meeting point of religion and the state insofar as they regulated political behavior and enforced social control even in the era of Americo-Liberian rule. In areas where they existed, no decisions could be made without the assent of leaders of the Poro.

The Poro was much more than a religious institution in that it exercised judicial powers, such as the trial of capital offenses and the imposition of commensurate penalties. Until the full establishment of central government control over the hinterland from the 1920s, the Poro and the chieftaincy institution worked hand in glove to administer those territories. Such was the importance of the Poro that the Americo-Liberian leaders from the 1930s courted it and sought to incorporate it into the system of government. As we have seen, Liberian presidents from D. B. King (1920–30) to Charles Taylor (1997–2003) got themselves initiated as members of the Poro and employed that leverage to entrench themselves in power. It did not matter that they were all professing to be Christians or even that Tolbert was a high church official. The manipulation of religion was a ready weapon of politicians lacking legitimacy and desirous of props for their regimes. As in the case of the Liberian presidents and the Poro, indigenous religious institutions and their functionaries have always been co-opted and incorporated into the political or administrative structure of the state to serve political ends.

Christianity and freemasonry also have been employed likewise, especially in the days of Americo-Liberian rule. From the start, the proclamation of Liberia as a Christian state on the model of the United States of America automatically co-opted the church in the goals of colonization and domination. The church was a willing ally because it needed the support of the state in the penetration of the Liberian hinterland, where it was encouraged to establish missions and educational institutions. Yet the church did not always enjoy a cordial relationship with the Liberian government. The revolts of the Grebo against the oppressive rule of the Liberian government were attributed by the government to instigation by the Christian missions operating among them. Consequently, the government became hostile to the missions and considered their activities undesirable. The missions were also accused of encouraging literacy in the indigenous languages at the expense of English, which was being promoted as a tool of national unity. Moreover, foreign missionaries working in the Liberian hinterland were also assumed to be responsible for reports circulating in the United States and Europe about the way the Americo-Liberians were maltreating the indigenous peoples.

Although relations between church and state improved from the time of President Tubman, tensions continued to characterize the relationship as the clergy often criticized the government from the pulpit. The church was a vocal critic of the corrupt and oppressive government of President Tolbert, especially in the wake of the rice riots and the government's ham-handed response to the popular discontent. When that government was toppled by the Liberian army, the church roundly condemned the arbitrariness of the Doe military regime, especially the summary trials and executions of members of the ancient regime. The churches were constrained to form the Liberian Council of Churches to serve as their mouthpiece in the face of the unabating despotism and barbarism of the Doe regime. The council constantly issued strong statements condemning the excesses of the government, and this prompted Doe to threaten to flog church leaders for engaging in so-called antigovernment activities. Doe also victimized the Methodist Church for its opposition to his misrule by withdrawing its tax-exempt and duty-free status.

RELIGION AND MEDICINE

A connection exists between religion and medicine on the one hand, and the peoples' worldview on the other. Each of the religions attribute most, if not all, ailments to the intervention of malevolent spirits, and they all share the approach of a spiritual solution to such problems. However, Christian missions pioneered and supported the application of *Kwii* (i.e., Western or orthodox) medicine to the various illnesses afflicting Liberian peoples. Yet it must be acknowledged that even the traditional and Muslim shamen also adopt certain universal medical practices, such as diagnosis (whether by divination or physical examination), application of herbs or herbal extracts (pharmacology), surgery (as in bone setting), and consulting.

In many Liberian communities, indigenous bone healers (*bilite* in Manding) apply orthodox medical practices—such as diagnosis or physical examination, massage, and psychotherapy—coupled with indigenous or Islamic incantations. Still, they refer difficult cases to more competent persons, just as Western medical practitioners refer complicated cases to specialist hospitals. In all cases, provision is made for alternative diagnoses and treatment, such that patients are taken from the indigenous practitioners to their Western counterparts and vice versa. This happens when people believe that their kinsman's or kinswoman's predicament (such as a motor vehicle accident) was caused by supernatural forces unleashed by his or her adversaries.

The intersection of religion and medicine is illustrated by the treatment of bone fracture, where the traditional physician not only offers a sacrifice before embarking on the treatment but also fractures the equivalent bone in a chicken or sheep that is given the same herbal treatment as the human patient. The sacrifice is expected to neutralize the evil forces perceived to have caused the accident, while progress in the treatment of the animal patient is used to measure that of the human patient.

Notes

1. Stephen Ellis, *The Mask of Anarchy: The Destruction of Liberia and the Religious Dimension of an African Civil War* (New York: New York University Press, 1999), p. 223.

2. The Sunnis are the mainstream or orthodox Muslims who constitute up to 90 percent of the total world population of Muslims. Shiites, who are found mostly in Iran and northern Iraq, differ on doctrinal grounds from the Sunnis. For example, they espouse the doctrine of hereditary leadership, that is, succession from father to son, and descent from the line of Ali, son of Prophet Muhammad's uncle, who moved the capital of the Caliphate from Medina to Baghdad.

References

Bledsoe, Caroline. "The Political Use of Sande Ideology and Symbolism," *American Ethnologist* 2, no. 3 (August 1984): 455–72.

Conteh, Al-Hassan. "Reflections on Some Concepts of Religion and Medicine in Liberian Society," *Liberian Studies Journal* 15, no. 2 (1990): 145–57.

Corby, Richard A. "Manding Traders and Clerics: The Development of Islam in Liberia to the 1870s," *Liberian Studies Journal* 13, no. 1 (1988): 42–66.

Ellis, Stephen. *The Mask of Anarchy: The Destruction of Liberia and the Religious Dimension of an African Civil War.* New York: New York University Press, 1999.

Fulton, Richard. "The Political Structures and Functions of Poro in Kpelle Society," *American Anthropologist* 74, no. 5 (October 1972): 1218–33.

Holsoe, Svend E. "The Dynamics of Vai Culture and Islam," *Liberian Studies Journal* 12, no. 2 (1987): 135–48.

Konneh, Augustine. *Religion, Commerce, and the Integration of the Mandingo in Liberia.* Lanham, Md.: University Press of America, 1996.

Korte, Werner. "A Note on Independent Churches in Liberia," *Liberian Studies Journal* 5, no. 1 (1971–72): 81–87.

Taryor, Nya Kwiawon Sr. "Religions in Liberia," *Liberia-Forum* 5, no. 8 (1989): 1–17.

3

Literature and Media

The Vai script has taken its own place among the advanced writing systems of the world, namely Arabic and English, both of which are alphabetic.[1]
—Mohamed B. Nyei, Liberian educator

The Liberian press has a legacy to live up to. It is perhaps the first attempt by Africans south of the Sahara to establish a press in the contemporary sense of the word.[2]
—C. William Allen, Liberian journalist

As A GENERAL PROPOSITION, it may be claimed that the volume of the literature and size of the media of any country reflect the rate of literacy and level of readership of its citizenry, access to educational facilities, and scope of the freedom of expression. The origins of literature and the media in Liberia may be traced to the establishment of the country as a colony of settlers in the 1820s. This chapter examines the development of the media and literature and their impact on Liberian society. The increasing rate of literacy and use of television and the Internet have combined to create greater awareness in Liberian society. To be sure, access to the Internet is severely limited to urban centers such as Monrovia, but even this development has also been affected by the upheavals in the country since 1980. Still, Liberians, like other people, have been influenced by the forces of globalization, not least the spread of a global culture via the Internet and cable television. This, as indicated in other chapters of this book, explains the intensification of the Westernization of Liberian dress, music, and culture.

LIBERIAN LITERATURE

Indigenous literacy and literature by Western-educated Africans in Liberia are of greater antiquity than in any other West African country. The principal reason for this is that the Americo-Liberian settlers came from a literate society and therefore transplanted American systems of education and writing to Africa. Yet they met an older tradition of scholarship in the Quranic system of education that came with Islam.

Islamic Literacy and Scholarship

As indicated in the previous chapter, Islam was introduced into indigenous Liberian communities through the agency of Mandingo traders and clerics at least as early as the eighteenth century. As the Muslim traders settled in various Liberian communities to carry out their commercial activities, they established Quranic schools and mosques for worship, training in Arabic, and religious instruction. Expectedly, Islamic religion and literacy in Arabic spread as Muslim traders expanded their commercial networks and settlements among the Vai, Loma, and Kpelle, in particular.

Arabic and Islamic education among the Muslim populations in Liberia stretches from the cradle to the grave. The pioneer Muslims doubled as traders and teachers and therefore established schools in their host communities. Such clerics, or *karamoko*s, invariably courted the local potentates, some of whose sons were thus inducted into the Quranic schools. Today, such children (and commoners' children, too) still enroll in Quranic schools, where they learn Arabic alphabets by rote. The *karamoko* writes the alphabets on a portable board belonging to each child and reads from the Quran with the pupils reciting after him. Though much of the time is devoted to such instruction, pupils also assist the *karamoko* on his farm or in his household. Each child is obliged to commit his or her lessons to memory, and the training is usually demanding, especially as corporal punishment is employed to reinforce the teaching and ensure the pupils' receptivity. Given this reality, many young Muslim children have to be compelled by their parents to attend the Quranic schools. As in other educational institutions, the Quranic schools are structured into several grades, with older students assisting younger ones. The pupils are taken through the Quran in four major stages, the completion of each of which is marked by the provision of a ritual meal for the teacher and pupils by the graduand's parents. The curriculum of the Quranic schools ensures that the pupils are able to read and memorize the Quran and then understand, interpret, and apply its various sections. It is also expected that accomplished pupils will be able to translate the Quran into their indigenous languages.

Quranic education is generally tasking and protracted. It takes as long as 11 years for the average child to attain the expected level of proficiency. Part of the reason for this is that the pupils combine their studies with service to the *karamoko* since they do not pay formal tuition. Hence, they spend about half the time on the *karamoko*'s farms and the rest on their studies. At the end of the course, the accomplished student has acquired mastery of the entire Quran.

Arabic and Islamic literacy has great utilitarian value in commerce and daily life. First, it confers an intellectual and social superiority on its possess-ors vis-à-vis their nonliterate neighbors. Second, such literati are thus able to serve as advisers to political rulers and other local notables. Third, the ability to communicate in spoken and written Arabic eases official and personal rela-tions and is valuable for conducting business and correspondence over long distances. Fourth, given that Arabic is the language and Islam the religion of commerce and diplomacy in the West African Sahel, Islamic education con-fers immense political and economic power and advantages as it connects the believer with a wider world of opportunities. Fifth, from the initial contact between the Guinea forest dwellers and Islam, Islamic *karamoko*s have been respected as diviners endowed with great magical powers. Hence, rulers and commoners approached them for help in preparing potent amulets and potions for victory in war or success in business. Usually, such amulets and potions were produced from particular verses of the Quran known only to those who are versed in them. However, the utilitarian value of Islamic educa-tion does not extend to the sphere of employment in the modern public ser-vice, for which literacy in English remains the principal prerequisite. This disadvantage is redressed somewhat, however, by the strategy of coupling Western education with the Islamic. Pupils are exposed to both systems of education, and in recent times Western-style Muslim schools have been estab-lished to provide Islamic education with the infusion of formal tuition in the core subjects of the formal curriculum. In such schools, Arabic is taught as a foreign language. This is a wise straddling of both worlds, but it is worth not-ing that, given the perception of Liberia as either a secular or Christian state, neither orthodox nor formal Islamic schools have received any substantial gov-ernment funding.

Indigenous Scripts and Literature

A significant aspect of Liberian history is the invention of indigenous scripts by several of its indigenous peoples.[3] The Vai, Bassa, Kpelle, Gola, Loma, Grebo, and Kissi all invented their respective scripts at various times in their histories. The Bassa script is said to have been invented by 500 B.C., though this assertion is possibly conjectural. Called Vah by the Bassa, meaning "to throw sign," it was meant to convey meanings through signs. Messages were passed through teeth marks on leaves placed at strategic positions where the recipient of the messages would read and decipher them. They were also transmitted through carvings on the bark of trees. This crude sign language was later codified in a complex written form. The Bassa script was taken to the Americas by enslaved Bassa (according to oral sources, by a man named Dirah and his partner, Madam Toeman, and developed by their son, Jenni Dirah) and passed from generation to generation. This New World survival (in Brazil and the West Indies) was discovered by Flo Darwin Lewis, a Liberian Bassa, who studied at Syracuse University in the United States. He launched a campaign for the revival of the Bassa script or alphabet (called *Ehni Ka Se Fa*) in Liberia. Though Lewis acquired a printing press for the script and established an institution for the study of Vah, he could not consummate his dreams before his death. However, the Bassa Vah Association rekindled interest in the development of the script for the purpose of publishing secular and religious literature, including newspapers. By the early 1970s, the Liberian Ministry of Education had formally recognized Vai and Bassa as written indigenous languages worthy of inclusion in the curriculum of the University of Liberia, but there were no personnel to teach the subject.

Far more celebrated than the Bassa script is the Vai script, the invention of which is widely acknowledged as a work of creative genius. Although accounts of its invention and development are often enmeshed in mythology, it is generally accepted that a young man known as Momolu Duwalu Bukele invented the script. He was said to have received inspiration for the achievement in a dream that he related to his friends, who encouraged and collaborated with him on the project. On a more tangible plane, it can be stated that Bukele's earlier sojourn on the Liberian coast, where he had experienced the impact of literacy, had induced him to work on the script, but the supernatural dimension might have added a spur to his aspiration.

Whatever the case, the invention of the Vai script postdated Bukele's return from the coast in 1819. After creating the script, he and his friends established a school at Dshondu for teaching the script, and this generated popular interest in it. However, interethnic wars of the early nineteenth century destroyed the schools that were set up at Bandakolo, Mana, and other Vai settlements, but the idea did not die. Although the schools were not resuscitated after the conflict, the preservation and spread of the script continued, and the process was accentuated by the work of another notable Vai personality, Momolu Massaquoi. A Western-educated Vai, in the 1920s Massaquoi exploited his position as superintendent of a school in the area to introduce Vai literature to his students. When the scheme expired with his tenure in 1929, another Vai,

Jangaba Johnson, reintroduced study of the Vai script in the local schools. These persistent efforts were rewarded in 1963 when the University of Liberia undertook the preservation of the Vai script.

Like other systems of writing, the Vai script has been developed and standardized by experts over the years. The script faithfully represents the consonant vowel structure of the language. However, it employs syllables rather than letters to represent words. The sounds of single characters or combinations of sounds of several characters are highlighted in the script to indicate the contextual meanings of Vai words. This naturally implies that one must be versed in the language to be able to use the script efficiently. By the 1980s, the Vai script had acquired a stable and generally accepted alphabetic system and had become so versatile that it permitted the translation of large sections of the Quran into Vai. This attribute has been exploited for proselytization by Muslim and Christian missionaries in Liberia. Muslim teachers have translated Arabic passages into Vai to facilitate their teaching, while the newspaper published by the Young Men's Christian Association (YMCA) contains a newsletter in the Vai script.

An important impact of the invention and survival of the Vai script is that it has produced a unique three-script literacy in a Liberian community. With the Arabic script deriving from Islam and the Roman script deriving from Christianity and Western civilization, the Vai script has contributed to a literary diversity unique not only to Liberia but to the whole of Africa. In a community where the large Muslim population has made Arabic a popular medium of writing and where literacy in English is also acquired by a significant number of young people, the Vai script serves much more than a supportive, sentimental purpose. During the 1980s, for example, it was discovered that the Vai script had been used in business and personal correspondence, including the keeping of accounts in business ledgers, and in the drawing of technical plans.

While farmers, craftspeople, and traders employ the script for business purposes, others have utilized it in recording family or clan histories, maxims, and folktales. Even the constitution and bylaws of religious associations have been documented in the Vai script. In a survey conducted about 1980, it was revealed that the Vai script was being employed principally in private correspondence and record keeping. It was also used to record minutes of meetings, house tax payments, details of public works, and death feast contributions. In the more technical matter of artisans' measurements and occupational requirements, the Vai script has been used to record customers' statistics for garment making, the number of cloth patches required for a dress, the number of bricks needed by masons for constructing a building, and dimensions of a carpenter's structural designs.

The Kpelle script was developed in the 1930s by Gbili, a paramount chief of Sanoyea in Bong County. It was said to have been revealed to him in a dream in the manner of the Vai script. As in the case of the other Liberian groups, such a supernatural origin gave credibility to the invention since, as noted in the previous chapter, dreams are highly regarded by Liberians. Unlike with the Vai script, however, the knowledge and usage of the Kpelle script were initially limited to the elite. Only privileged persons—chiefs and selected individuals, including one of Gbili's wives, Neni-tee—came to study and acquire mastery of the script. The script was popularized in the 1930s and 1940s as more persons passing through the strategic commercial center of Sanoyea acquired knowledge of the script. Till his death in the late 1960s, Chief Gbili and Lee-polu-mala-yale, a former clerk to Chief Gbili, encouraged its dissemination. The Kpelle script, like its Vai counterpart, was employed in record keeping, especially in relation to the inventory of stores and tax returns. Again, like the Vai script, it is a syllabary, whereby a symbol represents a syllable rather than a letter, and it is read from left to right.

The Kpelle script too has evolved since its invention in the 1930s. This explains the variations in the script over the area in which it is used, though these have been harmonized to a great extent. The emergence of the script appears to have been influenced by the prestige attached to the earlier indigenous and foreign scripts, but it did not imitate any one of them. Some minimal influence was drawn from secret mystical writings in Arabic. Like the Vai script, the Kpelle script was an entirely indigenous invention, the use of which is limited, however, to a dwindling number of persons given the greater utility of English and Arabic in official and commercial transactions in Liberia.

The Loma script was also invented in the 1930s by Wido Zobo, with the assistance of a few other persons. Wido too ascribed the invention to divine revelation through a dream and was assisted in devising the characters of the script by a weaver called Moriba. Like its Vai, Bassa, and Kpelle counterparts, the Loma script was used in personal correspondence, and its spread was facilitated by the prerequisite that learners of the script swear to their teachers to teach it to others. However, unlike the other indigenous scripts, it consists almost entirely of primary characters and contains very few diacritics to derive secondary characters.

The invention and usage of these indigenous scripts exemplify the capacity and dynamism of indigenous Liberian genius. Nowhere else in Africa is there such a concentration of indigenous scripts. But the demonstration effect of the Vai script—and the indirect spur of Western and Arabic literacy—on this development should also be acknowledged. That these scripts have not been adopted over wider geographic or cultural areas is the result of the overwhelming influence of the Roman script given its association with modern bureaucracy and statecraft in Liberia and the wider world. It is significant, however, that some of these scripts have been further developed beyond their initial invention and still serve some purpose in business and historical record keeping and in personal correspondence. Some have also been used to record folk tales and oral traditions of the respective peoples of Liberia. It is worth noting that the outstanding Liberian poet Bai Tamia Johnson Moore (1916–88) wrote at least one poem, "Maya I seneo," in the Vai script.[4] "The conception and elaboration of these scripts, and the practical use to which they have been put," it has been noted, "remain one of the cultural achievements of Africa."[5]

An important aspect of Liberian literature in the indigenous languages is the production of literary works in these languages written in the Roman script. Bai T. Moore epitomizes this trend. Born of a Vai father and a Gola mother, Moore was versed in both languages and produced high-quality poetry in them. Upon his return to Liberia from the United States in 1941, he wrote a poem in Gola ("Ko Bomi Hee M Koa") that recorded his impressions of his native land. A stanza of the poem is reproduced below in English:

Go tell my mother
To bring my root pot
To Bomi I'm going
Where I'll do my stuff
And sweat it out hard.

The determination of the returnee to work hard and his attachment to his African roots are conveyed in this excerpt.

Literature in English

The arrival of the Americo-Liberians in the 1820s signaled the formal indigenization of Western literacy in Liberia. The new type of literacy spread slowly, with the first formal school established in Robertsport in Cape Mount County in 1865, when Americo-Liberian clergyman Daniel Ware took some Vai boys and girls under his roof and instructed them in the English language. The establishment in the 1870s of the St. John mission by the Protestant Episcopal Church represented an attempt to Christianize the Vai, and it also marked a turning point in the spread of Western literacy in the Liberian hinterland. For the Vai in particular, St. John and its sister school Bethany mission proved to be the academic nurseries for virtually all of their leading Western-educated elite.

With the growth of Western literacy, Liberian literature in English flourished beginning in the nineteenth century. Possibly the most outstanding

Liberian intellectual and writer of that age was Edward W. Blyden, a notable Pan-Africanist in his own right. Allusion is made to him later in this chapter in his capacity as editor of a Liberian newspaper, the *Liberian Herald,* which he published more as a literary journal than as a disseminator of news. Blyden took up appointment as a professor at the University College of Liberia. A largely self-taught man, he generated seminal ideas about the plight of Black peoples, which constituted the fountain from which later Pan-African writers and thinkers such as Marcus Garvey, Kwame Nkrumah, Nnamdi Azikiwe, Sekou Toure, C.L.R. James, and Cheikh Anta Diop drew their own seminal ideas.

He can justifiably be described as the real Father of Pan-Africanism. Although he was Liberia's three-term secretary of state and ambassador to Great Britain, he still found time to study Islam and Africa's religious, cultural, and political ideas, which made him appreciate indigenous African religions and traditions in opposition to Western-sponsored Christianity. His book *Christianity, Islam, and the Negro Race* (1887) was a refutation of the orthodoxy of the age that Africa's salvation was contingent on dependence on the West and its dominant culture. Blyden made a powerful case for an autonomous, Afrocentric path to African development. He invented the idea, later popularized by Senegal's Cheikh Anta Diop, that Africa (specifically, Egypt) was the cradle of Western civilization, with Greece and Rome as the links between the ancient African civilization of the Nile Valley and modern Europe.

In subsequent years, a new crop of Liberian intellectuals and writers emerged as poets and literary writers. Bai T. Moore was an outstanding poet, novelist, essayist, and folklorist who was originally trained in the United States as an agriculturist and served in the Liberian bureaucracy on his return to the country. President Tubman later appointed him as an undersecretary of state for cultural affairs after a stint as a program officer for the United Nations Educational, Scientific, and Cultural Organization (UNESCO). Moore co-edited and contributed to *Echoes from the Valley,* a collection of poetry, authored *Ebony Dust* (1962), a volume of poetry, *Murder in the Cassava Patch* (1963), a story of betrayal, and *The Money Doubler* (1976), a social commentary; and contributed a story in *Four Stories by Liberian Writers* (1980). He collaborated with Jangaba Johnson, another notable Liberian writer, to publish *Chips from the African Story Tree,* a collection of Liberian folktales.

Given the range of his literary output, Bai T. Moore has rightly been described as the father of contemporary Liberian literature in English and, in a real sense, the embodiment of the county's cultural heritage. His poetry has appeared in international collections, some as early as the 1950s, and has also been translated into many languages. Moore's literary works cover the daily life of Liberians in urban and rural settings and even range beyond Africa to capture aspects of his own international experience. His literary works reflect on the travails of the masses, religious prejudice and hypocrisy, unrequited love, gender relations, materialism, and world peace.

Written in both pidgin and standard Liberian English, Moore's works address varying audiences in a generally accessible language. A vivid picture of the daily struggles of market women in prewar Liberia, which is still apposite today, is painted in his poem "Monrovia Market Women," written in pidgin, in a collection entitled *Grassroots*. In this poem and in his other works, Moore succeeds in highlighting the good and the bad, the beautiful and the ugly, the rural and the urban, and the sublime and the ridiculous. In "Sande Girl," he captures the pristine virtues of the young female initiate. His immense capability to cover a great variety of themes and terrain is unrivaled by any other Liberian writer. He is also able to communicate in easily accessible language (indigenous, pidgin, or Standard Liberian English) without obscuring the meaning of his poetry and prose.

Wilton Sankawulo, who served as chair of the Council of State of the Government of Liberia in 1995–96, is a novelist and professor of English literature at the University of Liberia. His publications include *Tolbert of Liberia* (1979), a biography of President William Tolbert, and two novels, *The Rain and the Night* (2001) and *Sundown at Dawn: A Liberian Odyssey* (2005). K. Moses Nagbe, also a professor of English language and literature at the University of Liberia, has captured the grim realities and the trauma of the Liberian civil war in his writings. Among his poems that recall the times of agony are "The Gods Rise, Thinking Through the Times," "Message from a Refugee," "Dividing Line," "Welcome Home," "Choppin," and "Down the Winding Road." The poem "The Gods Rise" reflects the mood during the protracted crisis of the 1980s and 1990s.

Patricia Jabbey Wesley, a professor of literature at Indiana University of Pennsylvania, is a rising Liberian female literary star who has made a mark as a poet of note. Educated in Liberia and the United States, she was a victim of the Liberian civil war, the recollections of which have featured in her poetry and other literary works. Her major works include *Before the Palm Could Bloom: Poems of Africa* (1998), *Becoming Ebony* (2003), and several scholarly essays.

In all, Liberian literature has been expressed in indigenous, Arabic, and Western (Roman) scripts. The literary production in each of these is of differing quality, magnitude, and utility. Both indigenous (Vai, for example) and Arabic scripts are better grounded in the village or rural setting, whereas English, being the official language of business, is better entrenched in public life (the formal economy, government, and public schools) and is therefore more of an urban phenomenon. Moreover, both Arabic and English have spread through the medium of religious institutions, though English has also exploited the avenue of public schools. The close relationship between Islam and the Arabic language has meant that mosques and Quranic schools, the network of trade, and the structure of village life have aided the spread of Arabic literacy in the rural areas of the Liberian hinterland. The Vai script lacks the institutional framework for dissemination that English and Arabic enjoy. Indeed, its spread and usage are more informal; there is no compulsion or material incentive for acquiring literacy in it. Also unlike Arabic and English, Vai is more localized among its indigenous speakers, for whom it facilitates interpersonal communication among spatially dispersed persons. All told, Liberian literature in any one of the languages compares well with the others. Writers of all manner of religious affiliations and academic attainments have captured aspects of Liberian life and culture in their poetry, prose, and historical writings.

THE MEDIA IN LIBERIA

The Liberian press is outstanding for its antiquity, being the oldest of its type in West Africa. It began with the contribution in 1825 of a sum of nearly $600 by the Massachusetts Colonization Society for the purchase of a hand-operated press in the recently established Liberian colony. The pioneer of the press was Charles L. Force, an African American printer and journalist who brought that hand-operated press to Liberia in February 1826. On February 16, 1826, barely 10 days after his arrival, he published the maiden issue of the *Liberian Herald,* which subsequently appeared as a fortnightly newspaper. However, his death only a few months after the *Herald* made its debut signaled the death of the pioneer newspaper. The *Liberian Herald* was revived in 1830 by John B. Russwurm, an émigré from Maine who had been a co-editor of *Freedom's Journal* in the United States. After taking up an appointment in Maryland County in 1836, Russwurm relinquished the editorship of the newspaper to Hilary Teage, who managed it till 1847, when the renowned scholar and thinker Edward W. Blyden took over and ran the *Herald* till 1862. From inception to the editorship of Blyden, the newspaper gave extensive coverage to news and events, but under Blyden it shifted focus from news to literary essays. This affected the fortunes of the newspaper, which gradually declined and died under Blyden's editorship.

Meanwhile, other newspapers had been established. The *Amulet,* the *Liberian Star,* and *Africa's Luminary* all debuted in 1839 but had mixed fortunes. While the others folded, the *Luminary* continued to appear twice a month for the next seven years. Surviving on subsidy provided by the Methodist Episcopal Church, the newspaper finally expired in 1846. Between the demise of the *Luminary* and the turn of the twentieth century, as many as 20 newspapers and magazines rose and fell. Among these were the *Liberian Advocate,* the *Liberian Sentinel,* the *Republican,* the *New Africa,* the *True Whig,* the *Weekly Spy,* the *Baptist Monitor,* the *Liberian Recorder,* and the *Monrovia Observer.* The last named was established in 1878 with the motto "Christian Liberia, open the door to heathen Africa."

The *Observer* was a vibrant paper that played effective watchdog and advocacy roles in late-nineteenth-century Liberia. Apart from championing education, temperance, the cause of Muslims, and the indigenous Liberians in the hinterland (known then as the tribes), it held public officials, including cabinet ministers, accountable for their deeds in office. Its editorials ventilated critical views of the emergent Liberian society and politics. The *Liberian Sentinel* and the *True Whig* were established in 1854 and 1868, respectively, by E. J. Roye, a successful businessman and politician who later became president of Liberia and whose tenure as president ended in tragedy and controversy. Both newspapers were short-lived and had been founded primarily to serve Roye's political ambitions.

Up to the last decade of the nineteenth century, Liberian newspapers had been the preserve of private entrepreneurs. But this changed in 1892 with the establishment of the *Liberian Official Gazette* by the Bureau of Information in the Liberian Department of State. As might be expected, it focused on the activities of government departments and news about the elite in society. The name of the newspaper was shortened to the *Liberian Gazette* in 1897.

Most of the nineteenth-century newspapers did not survive into the twentieth century. The places of the defunct ones were taken up by new ones such as the *Africa League,* the *Agricultural World,* and *Liberia and West Africa.* Possibly the most successful newspaper of the period was the *Liberian Recorder,* founded in 1897. Like the *Observer* in earlier years, the *Recorder* was from 1899 a standard newspaper with a clear focus and an appeal to a diversity of interests given its coverage of news and events of interest to the reading public. Surprisingly for a newspaper of its times, it strongly advocated the operation of multiparty democracy in Liberia by supporting the clamor for another party in opposition to the National True Whig Party, though the newspaper's chairman, T. W. Howard, had been a chairman of the ruling party. Nonpolitical causes championed by the *Recorder* were the development of cooperative farming, better prices for farmers, and other agricultural issues. As its name suggests, the *Recorder* distinguished itself by recording events in the evolution of Liberia and became a flourishing enterprise as it carried numerous advertisements. As a general-interest outlet, it created separate columns for diverse interests such as political, religious, racial, educational, and social issues, and it published letters to the editor that ventilated the views of its clientele. After experiencing fluctuating fortunes, the newspaper folded in 1906.

From the first decade of the twentieth century, the Liberian newspaper scene was dominated by *Liberia and West Africa* and the *Africa League*. Though the latter died in 1909, it had made its mark for opposing an attempt by President Arthur Barclay to amend the constitution to double the length of the two-year tenure of Liberian presidents. *Liberia and West Africa* was more enduring, surviving till the early 1930s. Published by the Methodist Printing Press, it was devoted essentially to the coverage of the mission's work, giving scant attention to the mundane issues that concerned the average reader. It was finally closed down in 1932 owing to disagreements over editorial policy.

The demise of *Liberia and West Africa* in 1932 was not an isolated event. During the years 1930–33, when the world was in the grip of the Great Depression and when Liberia was on trial by the League of Nations for the Fernando Po scandal, new newspapers flourished and perished. Among these were the *African Nationalist, African Watchman, Bensonville Whip, Crozierville Observer, Liberia Crisis, Liberian Patriot, Maryland News, Trumpet, Weekly Mirror, Whirlwind,* and *Youngmen's Literary Companion.* These newspapers were victims of the political and economic adversity of the times, poor management, and low numbers of subscriptions.

The newspaper industry in Liberia finally came into its own in the immediate aftermath of the Second World War. First, the postwar primary produce boom (rubber, palm oil, etc.) created a conducive atmosphere for its resurgence. Second, the watershed elections of 1943 and the resilience of opposition parties also facilitated the rise of newspapers with political affiliations. The *Liberian Age,* founded as a private venture in May 1946, began as a weekly but later became a biweekly that appeared on Tuesdays and Fridays. It soon became the mouthpiece of the ruling National True Whig Party. Opposition parties also established their own newspapers: the *Daily Listener, Independent Weekly,* and *Friend.* The *Listener* made its debut on May 22, 1950, as Liberia's first daily newspaper. But none of these publications could survive the hostile climate created by, and the strong-arm tactics of, the ruling party and its supporters. Between 1950 and 1970, other newspapers—the *Liberian Herald, Liberian Star, Palm Magazine,* and *Journal of Commerce and Industry*—were established, and they experienced mixed fortunes.

Liberian newspapers have experienced fluctuating fortunes since the nineteenth century. As with their counterparts in other areas of the world, they have had to contend with attempts to censor or intimidate them. But it was not solely a tale of woe for the press. The fact that some of the nineteenth-century papers could criticize government officials, champion independent causes with regard to national policy (for example, the treatment of hinterland peoples and temperance), and carry public opinion pieces indicates that the Liberian press enjoyed some degree of freedom during certain periods. Yet there were instances of intimidation of the press, censorship, closure of newspapers, and criminal prosecution of journalists. The printing press of the *Friend* was vandalized beyond repair; the editors of the *African Nationalist* and the *Independently Weekly* were sentenced to long terms of imprisonment for criminal libel of the political elite, including the president. The high-handed treatment of the press was based on an act of the Liberian government that imposed heavy punishment on anyone who libeled the president of Liberia or representatives of foreign governments in the country. The 1925 False Publication Act also stipulated heavy penalties for "harmful and false" statements against a person's fitness for office. The result for the press has therefore been cowed journalists and a culture of sycophancy. Journalists were thus restrained from offering critical opinions on the activities of government officials and other notables in society. Journalists convicted under the acts of 1924 (which prescribed penalties for criminal libel) and 1925 included C. Frederick Taylor of the *African Nationalist* (twice), and Bertha Corbin and Tuan Wreh of the *Independent Weekly,* who served prison sentences and were banned for a length of time from practicing their profession.

The long tenure of President William V. S. Tubman (1944–71) set the tone for media practice in Liberia for the rest of the period of Americo-Liberian rule. As a general statement, it can be asserted that Tubman actively discouraged journalism practice. As he faced imminent defeat in the presidential election of 1955, Tubman resorted to sheer gangsterism to cow the opposition and to muzzle the press. Independent newspapers were physically attacked by agents of the government, especially after a phantom plot was contrived to incriminate and jail the leading opposition figures. Treatment of the press was so heavy-handed that Liberian nationals feared to practice journalism. They opted for the safety of government service in the public relations department or took up jobs in areas outside active journalism. In any case, formal training in journalism was not provided in Liberia itself; a brief stint at the West Berlin Institute of Journalism was all that was available. Consequently, foreign journalists from other African countries, notably Ghana and Nigeria, filled the void. Though Tubman's successor, Tolbert, inherited this tradition of hostility to the independent press, he was more tolerant than his predecessor. Yet he too cracked down on the press and the opposition in the final year of his rule (1979–80), and this contributed to his downfall.

While this section has outlined the travails of the Liberian media during the period of Americo-Liberian rule, the situation after the April 1980 coup was hardly different. For the first time, Liberia was experiencing rule by one of the indigenous peoples of the hinterland and also rule by the army, worse still by noncommissioned officers. However, there was an initial euphoria engendered by the change and by promises of redress. For a time, bottled-up grievances were freely ventilated. During this period, the newspapers warmed up to the regime after its spokesman declared that the press had been granted "full freedom" to perform its functions without any inhibitions. But he added that journalists had to be "wholly and solely responsible" for whatever they wrote. This was an ominous hint that was lost on most euphoric Liberians at the time. Consequently, over thirty newspapers, mostly privately owned, emerged and flourished within the decade of Doe's rule and demise (1980–90). Eight of these specialized in sports coverage but most were short-lived. Of the large number of newspapers in circulation, only a handful—the *Daily Observer, SunTimes,* and *Footprints Today*—were truly independent. A few others appeared to have been set up to support the Doe government.

However, by September 1981, the Doe regime had begun to unfold its agenda of press censorship and soon clamped down on real and imaginary opposition. Its arbitrary and corrupt rule, and increasing insecurity owing to lack of legitimacy, predisposed it to clamping down on the press and other elements of civil society. The emergence of the *Daily Observer* (published by the veteran journalist Kenneth Y. Best and edited by Rufus M. Darpoh) in February 1981 set the stage for open confrontation between the Doe government and the press. In a series of news reports and editorials, the newspaper tested the limits of the government's proclamation of press freedom by highlighting some of the excesses of government officials. Like other repressive military governments, the Doe government harassed the *Observer* in many ways: it ridiculed and intimidated the publisher and editor of the newspaper, fined it for publishing a hostile article, deported its three expatriate staff, and shut it down five times. Its agents were presumably responsible for the arson that destroyed the premises of the newspaper in March 1990.

While the Doe government was having a running battle with the *Observer,* another newspaper emerged to check the government's excesses. This was *Footprints Today,* published by lawyer Momolu Sirleaf and edited at first by C. William Allen, which made its debut in March 1984. Like the *Observer, Footprints* too became a thorn in the flesh of the government, and its publisher and sports editor were accordingly detained without trial within six months of the newspaper's operation for publishing a supposedly offensive article. Both men were released after concerned Liberians prevailed on the government; they later sued the government for breach of their fundamental human rights. This earned them a further arrest and a 55-day detention in a notorious military camp. Rufus M. Darpoh, editor of the *Observer,* also suffered the same fate, in 1984, on the mere suspicion that he had written or

sponsored hostile publications in some foreign newspapers. Darpoh lan-
guished for six months in detention without trial in a remote military camp
meant for hardened criminals and was released only in response to intense
local and international pressure. He eventually moved on to edit another
newspaper, the *Sun Times,* published by Silvester Grisby, then a deputy minister of state in Doe's government. But the government invoked the notorious
antipress law, Decree 88A to shut down the newspaper for publishing a story
and an editorial on the presumed assassination attempt on the life of Baccus
Matthew, a presidential candidate and an opponent of Doe's in the controversial
1985 elections.

The Doe government did not stop at arrests and detention of journalists;
it carried out other forms of intimidation, including the public flogging of
the radio manager of the government-owned broadcasting corporation in
1981. Journalists were routinely assaulted by the police and government
thugs. Such was the level of physical assault that the Press Union of Liberia
formally protested in a 1986 statement the "constant harassment and intimidation" of journalists by security agencies. Such human rights violations were
backed by military decrees, however, especially Decree 88A of July 21, 1984,
which empowered security agencies to arrest and detain anyone engaged in
"spreading rumours, lies, and misinformation against any government official
or individual either by word of mouth, writing, or by public broadcast."
Though the decree was slightly amended in 1986 in response to pressure
from the press and the public, it was not repealed till 1990, after the fall of
Doe's regime.

The experience of the Liberian press under the Doe regime (1980–90) was
a litany of censorship, intimidation, arrest and detention without trial, and
murder. The mysterious death of broadcast journalist Charles Gbeyon was the
apogee of the excesses of the Doe regime against the press. The occasion for his
gruesome death was the unsuccessful coup d'état of Doe's erstwhile comrade
General Thomas Quiwonkpa, who had seized the radio station to proclaim
the presumed overthrow of Doe. But as the short-lived rebellion collapsed,
those who had appeared sympathetic to Quiwonkpa, including Gbeyon, were
summarily executed. In the case of Gbeyon, though he had no chance of
opposing the armed men who had invaded the radio station, he was brutally
arrested on Doe's orders while on duty and was later declared to have been
killed by an accidental discharge from a gun he was alleged to be carrying.

The conclusion of the Liberian civil war and the election of Charles Taylor
as president represented another phase in the history of the Liberian media.
The restoration of peace permitted the publication of as many as 10 newspapers in Monrovia, the capital, by 1999. There were also seven radio stations
in the country. However, both the print and electronic media faced great

challenges in the postwar years. First, the newspapers, except the one owned by the government, faced daunting financial, technical, and material handicaps. Bad roads increased the cost of distribution; the high cost of printing and the resultant high purchase prices limited circulation and subscription; and the low literacy rate in the country further limited newspaper readership. Second, given the repressive nature of the Taylor regime, the press came under state siege on several occasions, resulting in the closure of media houses and the harassment of journalists. Journalists faced subtle pressure, denial of access to information, and other forms of official hostility. The government in 1998 introduced stringent measures that had the effect of stifling the press. It stipulated that newspaper houses and radio stations must have a minimum deposit of $10,000 in their bank account before they could operate, and newspapers must achieve a minimum circulation figure of 4,000. Expectedly, the regulations were enforced selectively and vindictively.

The electronic media in Liberia comprise radio and television stations owned by a variety of interests. Among these (which were in place by the end of 1999) were Radio Veritas, owned by the Roman Catholic Church; Radio Star, funded by the Swiss; Liberia Communications Network, owned by the president; and the government-owned Liberian Broadcasting System, all of which, except those owned by the government or the president, encountered peculiar problems. The station owned by the president was the only one with the facility (shortwave frequency) to cover the entire country. Other stations had limited broadcasting hours or otherwise operated sporadically owing to the cost of operations, especially the burden of providing electric power from fuel-powered generators.

The government of President Charles Taylor closed Radio Veritas and Radio Star and disconnected the Internet service of the latter in May 2000, having declared them threats to public security. These outlets had apparently angered the government by producing phone-in programs that permitted citizens to ventilate their opinions on the government's policies and performance. Two newspapers, the *Inquirer* and the *News,* suspended publication in solidarity with the beleaguered radio stations. The ban on Radio Veritas was lifted after its management was made to sign an agreement to limit its broadcasts to religious matters.

In summary, the Liberian press has been under pressure from its early days. It has faced constant hostility from successive governments whose propensity for corruption, injustice, and oppressive rule has set them at odds with the press. Given the coercive power of the government—to make and enforce laws, both just and unjust—print and broadcast journalists have paid a high price for the practice of their profession. Those in the service of the government have had to engage in sycophancy or the dissemination of utter falsehood either to earn their keep or to escape the wrath of their paymasters. Where they attempted to be independent or fair, they incurred the wrath of agents of the state. In effect, the obsession with so-called state security—which means keeping the secrets about sordid deeds of government officials—has shackled professional journalism in Liberia. As we have seen, those who dare to be independent have risked physical assault, harassment, detention without trial, closure of newspaper houses, and death.

Moreover, the Liberian press has faced operational problems. First, the size of the economy and the private sector has been too small to generate sufficient revenue for the press from advertising. Because much of the advertising comes from government corporations, the manipulation of this source of revenue makes the independent press susceptible to economic reprisals by the government. The latter could exert pressure on or eventually cripple the critical press by withdrawing its advertising from hostile media houses. Worse still, private enterprises have also found it expedient to withdraw their advertising from such media organizations to curry favor with the government. Second, the rate of literacy (as low as 25 percent of the population) has also limited readership, a fact that combines with the weak revenue base of the press to limit its capacity. The average daily circulation rate of newspapers (1,000 to 10,000 by 1990) does not appear to make journalism a sustainable enterprise, even with substantial advertising revenue. It will take a higher circulation figure for the independent press to survive the onslaught of a hostile government's economic reprisals.

Third, media employees suffer poor working conditions, including relatively poor pay, which is consistent with the state of the economy and the media industry. As might be expected, journalists lack adequate facilities for reporting and producing news. Fourth, inadequate training facilities in the country, even with due allowance for the disruption occasioned by the war, have produced poorly trained journalists. Fifth, poor working conditions predispose media workers to inducement and intimidation, though these vices are not rife. Sixth, the protracted political crises have indirectly shaped the tone of media practice as more and more professional journalists have been compelled to join the political fray, thus eroding their independence. Political involvement has translated to greater partisanship, which may not augur well for the future.

These constraints notwithstanding, the Liberian press has fared well in the course of its long and checkered history. It has survived successive tyrants before and after 1980 and continues to be a credible source of news reports and analysis for Liberians at home and abroad as well as foreigners who are interested in the affairs of the country. Better training facilities have been provided with the establishment in 1983 of a department of mass communication at the University of Liberia. The department was established to award the four-year degree and a one-year certificate program in the discipline. Poor funding and a protracted political crisis have sorely affected its operations, but the department has managed to produce an admittedly limited number of graduates with degrees in broadcast and print journalism. The news media in Liberia are thus capable of fulfilling the universal mission of the media as the watchdog of government and society.

NOTES

1. Mohamed B. Nyei, "A Three Script Literacy among the Vai: Arabic, English, and Vai," *Liberian Studies Journal* 9, no. 1 (1980–81): 19.

2. C. William Allen, "Soaring above the Cloud of Mediocrity: The Challenges of the Liberian Press in the Nineties," *Liberian Studies Journal* 15, no. 1 (1990): 75.

3. A very good historical and in-depth analysis of these scripts is by David Dalby, "A Survey of the Indigenous Scripts of Liberia and Sierra Leone: Vai, Mende, Loma, Kpelle, and Bassa," *African Language Studies* 8 (1967): 1–51. Subsequent scholarly publications (Konneh, 1995; Stone, 1990; and Nyei, 1980–81) are also good supplements to it.

4. See Dorith Ofri-Scheps, "Bai T. Moore's Poetry and Liberian Identity: Offering to the Ancestors," *Liberian Studies Journal* 15, no. 2 (1990): 31. This source is arguably the most authoritative analysis of Bai Moore's writings.

5. Dalby, 51.

REFERENCES

Allen, C. William. "Soaring above the Cloud of Mediocrity: The Challenges of the Liberian Press in the Nineties," *Liberian Studies Journal* 15, no. 1 (1990): 74–84.

Brown, Robert H. "A Short Analysis of Bai T. Moore's Poetry and Prose Writings," *Liberian Studies Journal* 17, no. 1 (1992): 94–104.

Cole, Henry B. "The Press in Liberia," *Liberian Studies Journal* 4, no. 2 (1971–72): 147–55.

Dalby, David. "A Survey of the Indigenous Scripts of Liberia and Sierra Leone: Vai, Mende, Loma, Kpelle, and Bassa," *African Language Studies* 8 (1967): 1–51.

Hancock, Ian F. "Some Aspects of English in Liberia," *Liberian Studies Journal* 3, no. 2 (1970–71): 207–13.

Konneh, Augustine. "Arabic and Islamic Literacy in Twentieth-Century Liberia," *Liberian Studies Journal* 20, no. 1 (1995): 48–57.

Nyei, Mohamed B. "A Three Script Literacy among the Vai: Arabic, English, and Vai," *Liberian Studies Journal* 9, no. 1 (1980–81): 13–22.

Ofri-Scheps, Dorith. "Bai T. Moore's Poetry and Liberian Identity: Offering to the Ancestors," *Liberian Studies Journal* 15, no. 2 (1990): 26–90.

Rogers Sr., Momo K. "The Liberian Press Under Military Rule," *Liberian Studies Journal* 21, no. 1 (1996): 7–32.

Stone, Ruth M. "Ingenious Invention: The Indigenous Kpelle Script in the Late Twentieth Century," *Liberian Studies Journal* 15, no. 2 (1990): 135–44.

4

Art, Architecture, and Housing

The archetypical Gola artist is one who "dreams," and whose creative inspiration is supported by a very special relationship with a tutelary.
—Warren L. D'Azevedo, American anthropologist[1]

[T]he quest for status and having a good name is highly prized by artists of different ethnic groups in Liberia.
—Thomas K. Seligman, American curator[2]

LIBERIAN ARTS AND ARCHITECTURE PORTRAY the diverse experiences of the indigenous and Americo-Liberian communities. Housing types also reflect the cultural, social, and economic diversity of the people as well as the extent of external influence on them. This chapter draws examples from different historical and geographical contexts to illustrate the dynamism and versatility of Liberian artists and craftspeople. Although indigenous traditions in arts and architecture continue to survive, the pressure of external influences is relentless; the resultant combination has produced a uniquely Liberian arts and crafts tradition.

LIBERIAN ARTS AND CRAFTS

Traditional art consisted of various secular and religious pieces, the best known of the latter being masks of diverse sizes and cultural significance. Carving, painting, pottery, and weaving have been well-established crafts practiced by the peoples of Liberia from deep antiquity. Items produced by practitioners of these arts included metal ornaments, such as bracelets, rings, medallions, and chain necklaces; figurines for ritual and prestige purposes; decorated utensils, such as knives, bowls, spoons, and cups; and weapons. The Gola of western Liberia and the Dan (Gio) who live on both sides of the Liberia/Côte d'Ivoire border to the northeast have achieved great renown for their carving skills that have produced religious artifacts (such as Poro and Sande masks) and objects of secular utility. Mask carving was also practiced by the Vai of western Liberia, among whom the *sowei* mask was made, as in the territory of the Mende. The *sowei* masks were distinguished by their high-ridged hairstyle, a fashion that is no longer in vogue among Liberian communities, though the style was still represented on masks made in the 1980s.

Blacksmithing was a major art that also enjoyed great cultural and religious significance, especially in communities where the Poro and Sande existed.

Soapstone head, Kissi, from Sierra Leone, possibly seventeenth or eighteenth century. Although rare in sub-Saharan Africa, soapstone carvings are found in a small area that embraces parts of the modern states of Guinea, Sierra Leone, and Liberia. Most of the sculptures are of human form with some carved heads. © The British Museum/HIP/The Image Works.

Blacksmiths, who were usually male, employed the open mold, stamp pressing, filing and cutting, and the lost-wax process to make household utensils, weapons (spears and swords) and agricultural implements, and religious icons. They also repaired and sharpened cutlasses and knives. The art was transmitted within families and skills were acquired through an apprenticeship system. Among the Gola, blacksmiths enjoyed a higher status compared to carvers because they were admitted to the title of *zo,* a Poro position that bestowed wealth and prestige. However, the increasing reliance on imported household utensils such as spoons and knives has reduced the economic importance of blacksmiths. Yet the resilience of traditional agricultural practice, and its attendant reliance on hoes and cutlasses (machetes), has sustained the art of blacksmithing in the rural areas.

Spiritual explanations are generally offered for the unique gifts or talents of outstanding artists, especially carvers. The Dan believe that God (*Zlan*) was the first sculptor in that he molded human beings and animals out of the earth. Understandably, as we shall see in this chapter, people commonly attribute the talent of Dan and Gola carvers to a spiritual origin or inspiration. Among the Gola, the carver's genius is ascribed to an intense relationship between the carver and a powerful tutelary spirit of the opposite sex known as the *neme.* The love affair or relationship is said to be regulated by certain taboos or conventions, known as *negba,* that must not be violated. Woodcarvers and other artists who are reputed to be inspired by their *neme* are also assumed to be liable for paying a high price for their excellence, since they are believed to spend half their time in the spirit world. Such a relationship sets them apart from other human beings and is said to explain their unusual talent and unconventional lifestyle. In the making of masks for Poro and Sande, the Gola carver was secluded for the duration of the task. Even the women serving him food were not allowed to catch a glimpse of his carving while it was being done. Hence, the carver was bound to be a loner who was engrossed in his art and thoughts.

The Loma of northern Liberia are also renowned for their wooden masks. They made long wooden masks that contained human and animal features. Worn by men, the masks were associated with the Poro. The largest Loma mask known was about 5' 9" (1.82 meters) high, with a frightening visage accentuated by an exaggerated nose and forehead and a huge bunch of feathers attached to it. The Loma and their Bandi neighbors believe that masks represent the major forest spirit behind the Poro, called Dandai or Landa/Landai. In addition to this massive mask, numerous smaller ones have been produced by Loma carvers. They often have the horns of an antelope or cow above a flat face with a protruding nose.

Artists in Liberian communities give a higher premium to reputation than wealth, and that accounts for why they are not among the richest members of the community. A second common trend among artists, especially carvers, is their reliance on dreams as the source of inspiration for their work. As noted previously, they are believed to receive such gifts from a spirit helper called *neme* by the Vai and Gola and *du* by the Dan. Given this close association of artists with the spirit world, society tends to view them with a mixture of fear and suspicion, though their works are nonetheless admired. Indigenous Liberian artists are thus caught in a dilemma of nurturing their creativity to earn the respect of society or seeking to satisfy their own desire for individuality. Generally, carving is a product of natural talent that still has to be honed. Hence, though artists might claim some supernatural source for their talent, they still have to undergo tutelage under a master carver. Carving is a tasking pastime and is commonly associated with male members of the society. But women are known to have engaged in carving among the Dan, for example, though such breakdown of gender barriers is not widespread. Still, that trend, coupled with the stylistic changes in art forms over time, demonstrates the dynamism of the vocation. Changes in style have been caused by external forces like warfare, Islam, Christianity and Western education, and trade as well as the innovativeness of the artists themselves.

However, the pull of modernity, specifically, the demand for tourist art, has affected the quality of Liberian art. The need for quick service means that carvers have bent their skills to suit the customers' tastes, thus losing initiative to some extent. At least since the 1980s, artists began to make bigger and grotesque copies of previous artworks, a trend that has been called giganticism in African art. The more this trend persists, the farther away Liberian artists have been drawn from their original sources of inspiration in the indigenous society. In effect, unlike in traditional society, many Liberian artists have now yielded unconsciously to the lure of money, though this is not readily admitted. The autonomy that such artists used to enjoy in dictating to society what was art is now being lost as clients now dictate what the artist produces.

CARVING AMONG THE GOLA

Among the Gola, the woodcarver was as much a professional artist as the musician or weaver. Carvers, musicians, acrobats, dancers, magicians, storytellers, house decorators, orators, potters, and basket weavers were acknowledged as artists in indigenous Gola society. Woodcarving is a male preserve and the carver is called the *yun maku he* (one who carves wood). While all carvers have natural talent, it is usual for them to have undergone the process of apprenticeship, regardless of the claim by some that they acquired their skills through spiritual inspiration or the observation of master carvers at work. As mentioned earlier, the norm is for such persons (and even others) to attribute their creativity to the spirit force known as *neme.* Parents and elders watch out for signs of artistic tendency—as expressed in unusual dietary preferences, the tendency to emulate artisans, or an uncanny ability to master technical skills—in their children or wards. They give such children support if all attempts failed to dissuade them from pursuing a career in what was considered a strange and unrewarding profession. Hence, such budding talents are subsequently apprenticed to proficient carvers from boyhood.

As in Dan society, the woodcarver among the Gola is largely engaged in making masks for the Poro and Sande, a task that has great spiritual implications. Their training involves intensive apprenticeship and commitment of time and energy. Yet traditionally, the mask was a communal property to which the carver could not lay claim as a work of personal achievement; rather, it was generally regarded as the product of a supernatural maker. Most artists are also unable to amass much wealth or to earn the economic status that their talent ought to have bestowed on them. Even when Gola carvers are commissioned to produce a work of art, the credit for its excellence is given to the person "whose wealth and taste was responsible for the finished product, and not to the source of the workmanship."[3] Consequently, whether in the execution of sacred or secular commissions, the Gola carver tends to be anonymous.

There is sustained demand for the skills of Gola carvers, but this is focused on a few professionals and semiprofessionals who also have to move about or rely on commissions from patrons for their subsistence. The demand for their work is dictated by the religious calendar, the agricultural cycle, and the financial means of their clients. They sculpt in wood, metal, and ivory and make the musical instruments that many of them employ in their supplementary vocation as musicians. However, though Gola carvers are best known for their masks, they also make nonreligious objects, such as carved storage chests, figurines, toys, utensils, and decorative combs. They are often employed to decorate buildings and paint murals on walls for special occasions. Carving among the Gola has increasingly dovetailed with the related vocations of carpentry and furniture making. In this connection, the carvers have made the transition from carving porch posts for the elite to making ornamental household furniture, storage boxes, and doors. Under pressure from urban tastes and demands, the carver-carpenters have also been making replicas of traditional objects for urban consumers. They have employed modern tools to execute works that mimic the skills of the indigenous master carvers. The latter complain that works resulting from the new fad are hastily

A young man eyes a board to check to see if it is straight. He works as a cabinet maker for a nongovernmental organization (NGO) helping to construct a new village (July 2, 1997). © Mikkel Ostergaard/VISUM/ The Image Works.

and unprofessionally executed and have not been inspired by dreams as in the traditional context.[4]

THE ART OF THE DAN/GIO

Dan Wood Carving

The Dan or Gio of northeastern Liberia are outstanding carvers and sculptors; they are the counterparts of the Gola in the making of masks. Masks are acknowledged as the most important art form of the Dan/Gio, from which other forms of sculpture have emerged. They are important for their sheer number, being the most numerous single form of sculpture. Second, they have a spiritual significance that is universally acknowledged by most Liberian peoples. As discussed in chapter 2, many Liberians regard masks as the repositories of very powerful spiritual forces. Third, masks serve the political end of enforcing social control. Fourth, they are omnipresent instruments of socialization, being associated with major events in the community.

The central role accorded spiritual forces in the making of the mask is also reflected in the way it is carved and the use to which it is put. Masks are believed to be empowered by powerful forest spirits, called *gle,* that strive to embody any material object as a medium of its direct participation in the life of the community. Hence, it reveals to the carver what form the mask should take and the function it should perform. The dream is duly relayed to the council of elders, who authorize the making of the mask. As soon as he is commissioned, the carver makes the mask and other accompanying paraphernalia of the masked figure (e.g., fur, raffia, and feathers) to suit the character of the particular *gle.* Because each *gle* has its distinctive dance, personality, and speech patterns, there are as many masks as there are *gle.* Each mask is thus named after the particular *gle* that will possess it to reflect its individuality.

The *gle* and, therefore, the masks are of diverse forms and functions, though outward similarities can exist. The *gle* are given names that portray their supposed character. Generally, there are three kinds of *gle:* the *deangle,* which has gentle or feminine attributes; the *bugle,* the one with a warlike or masculine disposition; and the *gle va,* the great *gle* that can possess either tendency. The masks are accordingly carved to portray these attributes. Thus, the *deangle* mask has an oval face with graceful, feminine features, though the *gle* is supposed to be gender neutral. The fun-making *gle, weplirkirgle,* has a mask that matches its attribute: it has projecting tube eyes and distorted features that represent physical deformity. Yet it is not to be laughed at, even though it provokes people to laughter by its jibes at people with deformities. Anyone who laughs at its jokes pays a fine. It aims to reassure persons who are the butt of its jokes that they are not social outcasts. The *bugle* face mask has bold projections and portrays the fearsome martial qualities of the Dan. The dance that accompanies its appearance is vigorous and suggestive of masculine, aggressive behavior.

In addition to the large masks made by Dan carvers, small masks, called *ma go,* are made to represent spiritual forces known as the *du.* They are therefore made for the threefold ends of protecting their owners from sorcery, for divination, and for oath taking. *Ma go* masks are often smaller versions of full-sized masks that are reputed to hold spiritual power. In that case, the *ma go* is carried about as a symbol of the protection afforded by the bigger mask and a demonstration of the owner's status or identity. Hence, it is also known as the passport mask. Like the bigger masks, the *ma go* is given regular offerings of palm oil and rice, which are rubbed into it, as is the blood of chicken sacrificed on special occasions.

Feast ladles are objects of art that have social and religious significance among the Dan and their neighbors. The ceremonial ladle, known as *wunkirmian* or *wake mia,* is a large spoon carved in honor of women

(*wunkirlone* or *wunkade,* singular, *wunkirle*) who have distinguished themselves by their acts of generosity. Before and after her installation, the *wunkirle*
is noted for hospitality toward visitors regardless of their number or their
frequency of visit. She is therefore a hardworking and wealthy person in her
own right. Her wealth and generosity are displayed on festive occasions when
she leads a procession of women, her *wake mia* (ladle) in hand, to distribute
cooked rice and soup.

The ladles are carved in different shapes, usually with the head like a real
ladle (with a depression as the receptacle), but the handle is of different shapes.
Most handles have a human head, often replicating the face of the *deangle*
mask. Because the owner of the ladle is a woman, the carved human head is
covered with a hairstyle that is generally out of fashion in the community
(a result of the ladles being passed down from generation to generation).
Attempts are also made to make the handle of the ladle look as much as possible like the physical features of the *wunkirle* who owned it. In that case, her
hairdo, tattoo, and scarification are represented on the head carved into the
handle of the ladle. The handles of some ladles are also carved into the shape
of human legs, the torso joining it to the head of the ladle. The legs are said to
symbolize the number of guests that have benefited from the *wunkirle's* hospitality. Yet other ladle handles are carved into heads of animals, such as cows,
sheep, and goats, that are usually offered as bride price or as sacrifice at feasts.
The handle can also be carved into a small bowl that represents feasting or
provision.

Like the face masks, the ladle symbolizes not only honor and prestige but
spiritual power as well. The ladle is popularly believed to be the repository of
its owner's power, since it embodies her *du* and empowers her to become rich
and influential. Indeed, the ladle links her with the spirit world and is the
women's equivalent of masks for men. All ladles, like masks, are given names
to symbolize the attributes of their possessors. New ladles are carved to replace
old ones, but sacrifices have to be offered to induce the *du* to possess them.

Dan carvers also make wooden heads on a staff or other pedestals of various sizes. These guardian heads are taken to be receptacles of the spiritual
essence of dead persons or the embodiments of recently dead or living persons. These carved portraits of dead and living persons are believed to offer
protection and are therefore regularly propitiated through sacrifice. The
guardian heads are thus believed to be imbued with spiritual power.

Wooden human figures (*lime*) are also carved by the Dan, though with
less profusion than masks. These are ordinary secular works of art that have
been commissioned for their aesthetic value. The objects are as real as possible, with human features such as women's breasts, pregnancy, and hairstyles
fully represented on the carved figures. The faces are oval, the eyes have a

narrow slit, the neck has horizontal rings, and various forms of adornment are registered on the body: knee and ankle rings, ornaments, bracelets, and necklaces. In traditional Dan society, such art objects were commissioned by chiefs and wealthy persons or carved by the artists themselves. Chiefs and the wealthy paid for them in livestock or otherwise in kind and even held feasts to celebrate the completion of the contract. The objects were duly stored away as status symbols. If the artist had taken the initiative to carve the figure, he took it to the chief, who paid for it even though he had not commissioned the job.

Dan carvers also make gameboards for what the Dan and Man call *ma kpon* or *ma,* a game that is widely played across Africa. A board contains 12 round depressions carved in pairs into a sizable piece of tree trunk that is decorated with carvings of birds, snakes, and lizards. At each end of the board is a cup that is carved to contain the game pieces, made of the dried fruit of the *ma* vine. Often a human head or a ram's head is carved in place of the hollow cups at both ends of the board. Game boards are prized possessions that are passed down through generations in the family.

Metal Arts: Dan Brass Casting

Brass casting was a significant art of the Dan until the 1930s, when the Liberian government prohibited it. It has been suggested that the Dan learned the art from their eastern neighbors, the We, but opinions are divided on this claim. Brass casting and blacksmithing developed as related arts of the Dan since the brass caster was often originally a blacksmith. Both professionals were highly respected in Dan society, given the association of their art with ritual and spiritual power. Blacksmiths captured in war were spared and pressed into service for the community, which depended on their art for success in agriculture and warfare. Blacksmiths were often woodcarvers in their own right, as they had to carve wooden handles for their metal implements. As illustrated later in this chapter by the career of Ldamie, it was also relatively easy for a blacksmith-woodcarver to make the transition to brass casting.

Brass casting is a specialized field and its practitioners guard their skills jealously. Hence, they operate at night, when they can make their brass objects without letting out the secrets of their operations. Still, they take precautions against spiritual attack by keeping themselves spiritually pure—through abstinence from sexual intercourse; purging the heart of evil thoughts or malice; and keeping women away from their shop to avoid bewitchment, as women are generally associated with witchcraft—for the duration of time needed to produce a brass figure. Dan brass casters employ the *cire perdu* or lost wax method of casting brass figures. Initially, brass casters obtained raw brass from overseas trade with the Europeans and later, from secondary sources: brass basins, cannon barrels, and spent cartridge shells. Small brass figures of about eight inches (20 centimeters) in height were made to portray animals, such as elephants, dogs, and crocodiles, and changing styles of dress and armaments. These objects were metal counterparts of the carved wooden figures (*lime*) and were patronized or commissioned by the chiefs and the wealthy. A few exotic items, such as chairs and sandals, were cast in brass by Dan artists.

Brass jewelry, however, was by far the most important product of this art form. Necklaces, rings worn below the knee or around the ankle, and brace-lets were cast in brass in large quantities with variations in style. The bangles and bracelets were worn in a pile on the arms and legs, with those around the legs embellished with little brass bells. Women were saddled with rows of these relatively heavy brass rings, which added sparkle and class to their dress. Brass jewelry was added successively all through a woman's life and was worn until death. The increasing number and weight of the pieces indicated a woman's wealth, and her consequent immobilization reflected that she lived a life of relative ease while others worked for her upkeep. For this reason, that women were being hindered from productive work by the heavy burden of their brass ornaments, and for their supposed proneness to injuries and infec-tion, the Liberian government prohibited brass jewelry in the late 1930s. With the ban on brass jewelry, brass casting suffered a decline among the Dan. But it developed in another direction—the casting of human figures in brass, though in a limited number. Only a handful of experts emerged in this field, and the genre did not last long.

Outstanding Dan Wood and Metal Sculptors

Although modernity has made wood and metal arts less significant in con-temporary Liberian society, a point that is reflected in the relatively low num-bers of professional wood carvers and metal sculptors, the Dan produced renowned carvers and brass casters during the twentieth century. A man known as Zlan (meaning God) because of his uncanny ability to produce great artworks, is generally regarded as the greatest Dan sculptor who ever lived. Long after his death in the 1950s, his high reputation persists among the Dan and the neighboring We and Mano on both sides of the Liberia/ Côte d'Ivoire boundary. He was reputed to have had a natural talent associ-ated with some supernatural endowment portended by the circumstances of his birth. His father, a carver, died when Zlan was barely out of infancy, but the boy's prodigious talent was already manifest at the age of 13, when he produced his first mask. He subsequently became an outstanding carver of masks, ladles, walking sticks, rice bowls, stools, game boards, small spoons, and *lime*. Until he was incapacitated by a protracted illness that eventually proved terminal, he executed works commissioned by paramount and lesser chiefs, wealthy patrons, and others. Like other Liberian artists, Zlan drew his inspiration from dreams in which he reportedly received instructions from his dead father to create new art forms, such as a new type of mask known as the *blokila* (a mask with two projecting cow horns) and the Janus-type of feast ladle. He was well paid and honored for his works and was bestowed with gifts of wives and material objects. One of his wives became an accomplished carver in her own right—a departure from normal practice among the Dan.[5]

Zlan shared his knowledge with others by teaching generations of apprentice carvers who came to his base at Belewale in northeast Liberia. Among his apprentices were those who came to watch him and work under his supervision for a few days, and those who stayed for much longer to gain mastery of the craft. There were also those who were sent by their chiefs to understudy Zlan so that their communities too could have resident master carvers like him. The apprentices helped cut the tree trunks required for carving, worked on his farms, and did preliminary carving that the master himself perfected. They aimed to imitate Zlan, and their success was judged by their ability to replicate his style of carving. Zlan's students maintained contact with him after their graduation and demonstrated their gratitude to and respect for him by sending occasional gifts.

One of Zlan's outstanding students was Zon, who was originally a master blacksmith. After an initial encounter in the late 1940s, Zon began making tools for the master carver.   He later became an apprentice carver and soon became accomplished in his own right. The first mask that he carved under Zlan's tutelage was a masterpiece and in subsequent years became much sought after among the Dan of his clan and their neighbors. Like Zlan, Zon too produced many masks, feast ladles, *lime,* and game boards. He became famous for carving a distinctive face on his ladles and human figures, with the women having a herringbone style coiffure.

Zlan died in the early 1950s and Zon in 1985, and their art would appear to have declined with their passing. Younger carvers such as Dro, a grandnephew of Zlan, have been more flexible in the execution of their works in terms of their responsiveness to the pull of the market and modernity. Dro innovated to meet the demands of tourists and foreigners who were interested in exotic art that did not necessarily represent indigenous Dan or Liberian traditions.

Zlan's counterpart in metal arts was Ldamie, who distinguished himself in brass casting. Ldamie was born into a family of brass casters in Zonleh in northeast Liberia in approximately the first decade of the twentieth century. Like other brass casters of his generation, he was first a blacksmith but became a carver before transforming into a brass caster. Between the 1920s and the 1950s, he produced a large number of brass swords, gun handles, sword handles and sheaths, bells, jewelry, animal figures, and fly whisk handles. Ldamie had cast figures of chiefs and wealthy persons in brass before a chance encounter with a Liberian government official provided a wider vent for his talent. He then secured many contracts to make brass figures of government officials, which brought him great wealth, fame, and honor.

The aforementioned Dan artists worked in wood and brass, and their works exemplified innovativeness and creativity. They achieved fame and accumulated wealth, though their large families and the vagaries of patronage meant that they also had to earn supplementary income from farming. Though they made human figures in response to contracts awarded by their patrons, they also represented animals and other objects in their works. However, the pull of modernity means that younger artists such as Dro have had to relate their talent to the demands of a new market—tourism and the urban elite. This has robbed their works of the authenticity of the older generation of artists, but their works are nevertheless Liberian in conception and execution in that they are variations on the older art forms.

BODY ADORNMENT AS ART

Representations of human figures or attributes in the art or body adornment of Liberian peoples suggest their idealized form of beauty. The Dan or Gio *deangle* masks portray the people's conception of beauty: slit eyes, which barely show when the eyelids are lowered; an oval face; a little glimpse of the incisor teeth between the lips; tattoo markings on a vertical pattern on the forehead; and kaolin decoration around the eyes. Old Dan masks have raised tattoo markings in a vertical order on the forehead, a form of adornment practiced by women in traditional society. But that practice is no longer in vogue among the modern Dan of Liberia. However, young girls in the rural areas still practice a variant of this adornment by applying white kaolin paint in a narrow band across the face between the eyebrow and the bridge of the nose.

In contemporary times, body painting of a different type is done by urban dwellers or Western-educated women. The fashion tastes of such modern women are influenced by those of the West and are patterned after the styles of famous American, European, and African film stars or musicians. Artificial eyelashes and fingernails are added for effect; the hair is stretched and shaped into various styles through a process called hair perming; and more exotic hairstyles, such as Bob Marley dreadlocks, are adopted. However, bleaching of skin is not as widespread as in other West African countries. Young men emulate the dress and hairstyles of soccer and music stars in Africa and beyond. Modern youth dress culture is predominantly informal, with blue jeans being the most popular.

The weaving or styling of men and women's hair is a great work of art among all Liberian communities. Women's hair is plaited in the open by relatives or professional stylists. In many rural Liberian communities, it is unconventional for women to go out without a head covering. This is a paradox because underneath the scarf or head tie is a great work of artistry. Women's hair is braided or plaited in diverse ways in accordance with their age or status. Generally, women of high status who can afford the luxury make elaborate braids that are numerous and small in size. These usually take several hours to make, depending on their complexity. But whereas older or very busy women may not have the patience to sit for a stylist for so long, younger women with an eye toward aesthetic appeal to suitors readily endure the strain. They also embellish their hair by adding material for its artificial elongation because long hair is generally fancied by men and women in African societies.

WEAVING

Although the indigenous textile industry has faced the relentless onslaught of foreign textiles—new and secondhand—it still serves a substantial market in the rural and urban areas. This is a consequence of lingering pride in indigenous culture, especially dress. Indigenous cloth is produced by a variety of looms—the narrow strip treadle loom, the vertical loom, and the ground loom. Various Liberian peoples—the Vai, Mandingo, Mende, Kissi, and Gola—have distinct weaving traditions and looms for producing cloth of various designs. Generally, these peoples produce what is called country cloth, or *kpokpo*, of a great variety. Indeed, no two cloths are exactly the same because the weaver displays ingenuity to produce a unique item on each occasion. Hence, both designs and colors are varied, but general patterns are discernible over a particular geographical or cultural area.

Gola weavers (*anyun juwa de*), like their Vai, Kissi, and Mende counterparts, produce country cloth of various designs. Weaving, like carving and blacksmithing, is a male preserve that lacks the charisma or spiritual attribution accorded carving, though it is an important vocation in its own right. Though assailed by imported textiles, country cloth produced by Gola weavers enjoys a stable demand for its exotic value as prestige objects—it is fashioned into either ceremonial robes for the indigenous elite or gift items presented to visiting officials. High-quality cloth for these purposes is made from indigenous cotton cloth woven with local cotton spun by women. Men weave the yarn on horizontal looms into long narrow strips that are then sewn into gowns, blankets, and rugs. Woven material large enough to make a man's gown requires work of at least three weeks. Like carvers, weavers also depend on commissions, which take them far away from home. This is a departure from the traditional practice whereby weavers were attached to affluent families and only the best could attract commissions from other places. But with the development of a modern economy, it is no longer possible to sustain the indigenous type of patronage (an accompaniment of a sedentary agricultural socioeconomy), especially given that fewer persons are engaged in weaving. The master weavers now tend to send their apprentices to handle commissions rather than travel themselves.

Textile designs among the Gola are generally standardized. Apprentices tend to follow the patterns of their masters even after graduation, or they copy older designs. Still, there are innovative weavers whose designs are attributed to inspiration received from their *neme* through dreams. One such master weaver faithfully recorded the revealed designs in a notebook and never repeated a major design except at the insistence of a client. His reputation was widespread, and even his apprentices attributed their own designs to him so that their deviations from the traditional norm could be legitimized.[6]

The great variety of indigenous cloths produced by Liberian peoples and their neighbors consists of several categories, including the weft-dominated, checkerboard designs, and composite cloths.[7] The *stepi* design (so called because the design looks like a set of steps) is characteristic of Gola and Vai weaving. As in carving, Gola weavers rely on dreams or inspiration to fashion out new *stepi* designs in intricate geometrical patterns. Those designs are sketched out on paper and then implemented by the weavers. The Vai, on the other hand, have developed the checkerboard designs on the pattern of the boards used to play checkers or draught games, as well as composite designs that incorporate several distinct designs. Liberian peoples specialize in making specific types of cloth, though those styles have increasingly diffused across ethnic frontiers. The Mende are associated with the warp stripe pattern, which has a parallel in Kissi cloth, though the latter is woven in a tighter fashion. Kissi weavers tend to experiment more with chemical dyes, which produce a variety of colors, than any of their neighbors. This has enabled them to produce brightly patterned cloth of jet black, bright orange, and dark green. A particular style of Liberian textiles incorporates writing (e.g., a proverb, the name of a chief or a motto) into the woven design, especially to commemorate an occasion.

A point worth noting is that cloths served different purposes—as everyday wear, ceremonial apparel (e.g., for wedding, Poro graduation, or chieftaincy installation) and funerary cloth. Cloths could be light or heavy, narrow or large. Light cloth was used to make women's under wrappers or head ties while heavier cloth served as outer wrappers (*lappa*). The latter could contain as many as 14 strips and measure almost six feet (two meters) in length. Heavy cloth was also used to make cover cloths, which served as a form of blanket. On state occasions, traditional cloths are spread on the high table for dignitaries, a practice that was begun in nearby Sierra Leone.[8] A noticeable development has been the tendency for weavers to produce wider strips so that fewer strips are joined to make cloths such as the *lappa*. Moreover, hand-spun yarns have been displaced to a large degree by machine-spun yarns.

Weavers are generally commissioned to produce a particular design, often for a wealthy patron or chief, and for certain ceremonies. Weavers can operate chiefly under patronage or establish themselves as independent artisans. The color patterns can be woven directly into or stamped on the material. Factory-produced yarns are used to weave colorful patterns. In addition to cloths, mats are also woven by Liberian peoples for use as beds, room dividers, and screens. These mats as well as bags are made of material from raffia palms, which abound in the West African region. Raffia bags of various sizes and colors are produced as a supplement to cloth weaving, though the creativity involved is not necessarily inferior. The Liberian rice bag, a seamless cylindrical receptacle made of raffia, is an outstanding work of utilitarian art. The seamlessness of the bag symbolizes both perfection and wholeness. Contrary to the connotation suggested by its name, the bag can be used to carry any tangible items, such as clothing and other personal effects. The bag is serviceable and can be folded and reused several times over. The production of the Liberian rice bag is the domain of men. The rice bags made an impression on American Peace Corps volunteers in the 1960s, and their penchant for using them as purses popularized the bags as the "Peace Corps bag" or "Peace bag."[9]

ARCHITECTURE AND HOUSING

Liberians live in a wide variety of types of houses depending on their location (urban or rural), family size, social status, and economic status. Traditional architecture, consisting of houses and bridges, can still be seen in many rural communities today. Many communities are linked by suspension bridges constructed across rivers and streams, which become impassable because of flooding during the rainy season (April to November). Such bridges are made of tree trunks and other forest materials. In rural communities, houses are built with two common features: a circular structure and a conical roof. The roof is made of palm fronds and a special grass that grows on hilltops.

The making of the roof is an art in itself in that the product keeps out water during the torrential rains that fall during the rainy season. The roof is slanted so that it drains the rainwater no matter the intensity of the rain. Although the material used in roofing is easily combustible, it creates a cool ambience inside the house. The indigenous house often stands on wooden pillars and generally on mud walls. From at least the middle of the twentieth century, grass roofs have given way to iron roofing sheets, even in places outside the major urban centers. Many mud houses have assumed the square rather than circular shape. Traditional Kpelle and Bassa houses are rectangular while Gio's are circular.

Houses in the urban centers of Liberia, especially the capital, Monrovia, are of a different style. The settlement of the Americo-Liberians in the 1820s introduced Western-style architecture to Liberia. The settlers simply transplanted Southern U.S. architecture to their new homeland. The affluent settlers constructed two-story houses that consisted of a stone basement and a wood-frame body with front and rear porticoes. Joseph Jenkins Roberts (1809–76), Liberia's two-term president (1848–56, 1872–76) and a wealthy merchant in his own right, built an impressive private residence in Monrovia. The official residence of the Liberian president was a stone mansion modeled on the American Southern plantation house. Other Americo-Liberian houses of the nineteenth century were likewise patterned after the plantation manor houses of the pre–Civil War era in the American South, complete with their tall-columned entrances. The interiors of the houses were furnished in the

Gola house, 1900. Courtesy of the Library of Congress.

style of the typical American Southern Black household, with paintings of pets and displays of china plates and cups. The elite Americo-Liberians in Monrovia had more elaborate furnishings.

In the 1920s, Afro-Brazilian architectural styles were introduced into Liberia. Since the mid-twentieth century, the modern style of architecture common to the surrounding former European colonies has become prevalent in Liberia. Single- and multiple-story residential and office complexes of various designs made of reinforced concrete and mortar can be seen in Monrovia and in other urban centers. Prewar Monrovia contained public buildings and private residences of high architectural and aesthetic quality, including the Capitol, the Executive Mansion, City Hall, the John F. Kennedy Hospital, the Fendall campus of the University of Liberia, the E. J. Roye building, and the Temple of Justice. Winston Richards (1932–2002), a renowned Liberian architect, was involved in the design and construction of many of the public buildings in Liberia between 1958 and 1980, when he held key posts in the ministry of public works. Marble and glass buildings of grandiose proportions were constructed in Monrovia under the rule of President Doe in the 1980s.

Places of worship are among the most impressive architectural sites in the country. Magnificent church buildings and mosques, such as the Providence Baptist Church in Monrovia (built in 1839) and the central mosque in Gbarnga, abound across the country. They reflect the people's attitude to religious congregations and their commitment to building appropriate

Dingamo village boys making mud blocks, c.1956. Courtesy of the Library of Congress.

President Robert's House, Monrovia. Courtesy of the Library of Congress.

Executive Mansion. Courtesy of the Library of Congress.

edifices as places of worship. However, many of these buildings were vandalized during the political crisis and civil war of the 1980s and 1990s—indeed, an infamous massacre took place in a Monrovia church—though postwar rehabilitation has achieved appreciable progress.

Urban houses in Liberia range from apartments and townhomes to private mansions, depending on the financial circumstances of their owners. Mortar has become the dominant element in constructing or plastering the walls of houses, while the roof is made of a foundation of wood (planks) and a cover of metal or asbestos roofing materials. The modern real estate industry is relatively small and urban focused; it provides employment for masons, house-painters, interior decorators, and carpenters. Houses are painted in diverse colors according to the taste of their owners. Yet it must be noted that in cities such as Monrovia, there are shantytowns, unplanned and densely populated neighborhoods, where people live in crowded tenements without conveniences such as toilet facilities or potable water. Life in such depressed neighborhoods has been captured in the literature, as demonstrated in Bai T. Moore's poetry in chapter 3. The situation has been compounded by the protracted civil war in Liberia, which ruined much of the existing urban and rural housing and other infrastructure.

NOTES

1. Warren L. D'Azevedo, "Sources of Gola Artistry," in *The Traditional Artist in African Societies,* ed. Warren L. D'Azevedo (Bloomington: Indiana University Press and International Affairs Center, 1973), p. 335.

2. Thomas K. Seligman, introduction to *Four Dan Sculptors: Continuity and Change,* by Barbara C. Johnson (San Francisco: The Fine Arts Museum, 1987), p. xiv.

3. K. Peter Eztkorn, "On the Sphere of Social Validity in African Art: Sociological Reflections on Ethnographic Data," in *The Traditional Artist in African Societies,* ed. Warren L. D'Azevedo (Bloomington: Indiana University Press and International Affairs Center, 1973), p. 365.

4. D'Azevedo, "Sources of Gola Artistry," p. 326.

5. Johnson, pp. 36–37.

6. D'Azevedo, "Sources of Gola Artistry," p. 328.

7. Venice and Alastair Lamb, *Sierra Leone Weaving* (Hertingfordbury, United Kingdom: Roxford Books, 1984), p. 104.

8. Ibid., chapter 14, figure 116 (unpaged).

9. Esther Warner Dendel, *African Fabric Crafts: Sources of African Design and Technique* (New York: Taplinger, 1974), pp. 154–56.

REFERENCES

Boone, Sylvia A. *Radiance from the Waters: Ideals of Feminine Beauty in Mende Art.* New Haven, Conn.: Yale University Press, 1986.

D'Azevedo, Warren L. "Mask Makers and Myth in Western Liberia." In *Primitive Art and Society,* ed. Anthony Forge. London: Oxford University Press, 1973, pp. 126–50.

D'Azevedo, Warren L. ed. *The Traditional Artist in African Societies.* Bloomington: Indiana University Press and International Affairs Center, 1973.

Dendel, Esther Warner. *African Fabric Crafts: Sources of African Design and Technique.* New York: Taplinger, 1974.

Fischer, Eberhard. *The Arts of the Dan in West Africa,* trans. Anne Buddle. Zurich: Museum Rietberg, 1984.

Himmelheber, Hans. "Sculptors and Sculpture of the Dan." In *Proceedings of the First International Congress of Africanists,* ed. L. Brown and M. Crowder. London: Oxford University Press, 1964, pp. 243–55.

Holsoe, Svend, and Bernard L. Herman, *A Land and Life Remembered: Americo-Liberian Folk Architecture.* Athens: University of Georgia/Brockton Art Museum, 1988.

Johnson, Barbara C. *Four Dan Sculptors: Continuity and Change.* San Francisco: The Fine Arts Museum, 1987.

Lamb, Venice, and Alastair Lamb. *Sierra Leone Weaving.* Hertingfordbury, United Kingdom: Roxford Books, 1984.

Levy, Patricia. *Liberia.* New York: Marshall Cavendish, 1998.

Phillips, Tom, ed. *Africa: The Art of a Continent.* Munich: Prestel Verlag, 1995.

Sieber, Roy, and Frank Herreman, eds. *Hair in African Art and Culture.* Munich: Prestel Books, 2000.

5

Cuisine and Traditional Dress

[M]any of us in Liberia have been misled into believing that eating "pussava" or Uncle Ben's rice makes us "kwi" (civilized) people instead of seeing our dependency...as self-enslavement.
—Syrulwa Somah, Liberian professor[1]

In older times in Liberia, the simple act of wrapping a length of cloth, lappa, about the torso, was a sacred and prayerful beginning to a new day.
—Esther Warner Dendel, artist[2]

DRESS AND CUISINE PROVIDE important indicators of the personality and character of a people. As detailed in this chapter, the great variety of Liberian cuisine projects the blend of indigenous and foreign elements and influences in the making of the country's food culture. In addition, men's and women's clothing, appropriately designed to be loose fitting; the styling of the hair; the fashionable designs of headgear for men and women; the elaborate embroidery on men's and women's flowing gowns; and the assortment of colors project the people's penchant to enjoy life and make the best of their circumstances. This uncanny ability to give meaning to their existence and to enjoy life to the fullest characterizes the culinary and sartorial lifestyles of Liberians, as it does for other Africans.

Changes have taken place in the composition of the cuisine and the hair and dress styles of the peoples of Liberia. Although elements of indigenous cultures are dominant in these aspects of life, foreign influences have become increasingly influential. What emerges in each case is an amalgam of both tendencies and the adaptation of foreign cuisine and dress styles to the local context. In both food and dress, Liberians have proven to be innovative, responsive to external dynamics, and adaptable to changing circumstances—while retaining the essence of their indigenous traditions. This does not diminish the impact of foreign food imports and the influx of new and used foreign textiles. Youths and other urban dwellers have been most vulnerable to foreign influence in dress and cuisine. Fast food and blue jeans, respectively, epitomize the pervasive influence of globalization on Liberian food culture and dress styles.

CUISINE

Like other West African nations, Liberia is endowed with a blend of traditional, Western or foreign, and hybrid cuisine. In the Liberian case, the distinction of a formal noncolonial past has not made the people and their food customs immune to foreign influences. Generally, Liberian cuisine comprises the indigenous food customs of the various ethnic groups in the country, the hybrid cuisine of the Americo-Liberians, and foreign imports. Food is determined by class or status and economic means. A well-fed person is one who has a stout or rotund stature, regardless of the risk of obesity. As is detailed in this section, Liberian cuisine is diverse and rich, drawing from the diversity of the country's ethnic composition and historical experiences.

Though Liberian cuisine is rich and varied, most dishes contain one or more of several key ingredients—palm oil and other vegetable oils, fish, cassava, and pepper. Unlike many people in the West, Africans, including Liberians, like their meals prepared with a generous portion of hot pepper. A characteristic of the Liberian food repertoire is the versatility of the people in making several kinds of dishes from a single item. Cassava, for example, is processed into food by grating or pounding it into pulp or by boiling, baking, or grilling it before consumption. This gives the people a variety in their diet and allows them to complement the starchy content of the cassava with other more nutritious condiments.

Unlike most people in the West, Liberians generally cook their meals at home, but public eating houses exist to cater to the needs of unmarried people or wage employees who might not have the time or desire to prepare their own meals. Known as cook shops, such low-cost, lower-class restaurants offer many of the dishes described previously. Some of the most popular dishes are *jollof* rice, goat soup, and check rice. Public eating houses and fast-food outlets are sited at strategic locations near markets and motor parks, where the concentration of people is expected to ensure heavy patronage.

Liberians observe certain food taboos and conventions. Many meals are eaten with the fingers, but the hands have to be washed before the food is eaten. Moreover, one does not eat with the left hand, which is considered inferior to the right hand since it is used to clean up in the toilet. As well, food must be properly covered while being cooked and served to prevent infection and the outbreak of epidemics. Hence, the most scrupulous standards of cleanliness are required of women who cook and serve meals. The best plates are used to serve meals to visitors, who are accorded the highest regard according to indigenous standards of hospitality. Usually, provision is made for unexpected guests, and no family ordinarily cooks just enough for its immediate requirement. As indicated in chapter 2, various communities observe food prohibition according to religious or cultural beliefs. Muslims do not eat pork or drink alcoholic beverages. Totem animals or ritually prohibited animals, such as monkeys, are forbidden to certain categories of persons for religious or ritual purposes.

However, imported food has become more important in the diet. Indigenous rice (called *bogaa* in Kru and Bassa languages) has been largely displaced by imported brands, especially as urban Liberians have taken to using parboiled rice from the United States (e.g., Uncle Ben's) and Asia. This decision was probably informed by the assumption that the imported brands were more nutritious, a claim that is dubious. It is significant, however, that the crisis surrounding rice imports, a business alleged to have been controlled for huge personal profit by Liberian leaders, led to the ultimate fall of the Tolbert Americo-Liberian government in 1980. Apart from imported rice, many foreign delicacies have permeated the Liberian diet, especially in urban areas. Processed vegetable oil, sardines, Irish potatoes, and frozen chicken from various Western countries have virtually displaced coconut, peanut, corn, and palm oil, which were indigenous staples. Like its West African neighbors, Liberia, even in prewar times, had gradually neglected its food crop economy and had become increasingly dependent on foreign imports, with political repercussions. The war displaced large populations and affected agricultural production. There was food scarcity, even to the point of famine, and the country has yet to fully recover from the ravages of the war.

Liberian Soups and Stews

Liberian soups contain a blend of vegetables, okra, string beans, fish, and meat. Ingredients for beef soup, served with rice and *foofoo* (a special type of meal derived from processed cassava), include fresh tomatoes, onions, salt, tomato paste, beef, dried codfish, smoked fish, black pepper, and coarse red pepper. Stewed mango with cloves is a fruit dessert taken with dinner or served separately. It can also be created from fresh or canned stewed peaches or apricots in the absence of mangoes, with the fruit being peeled and cut in large pieces. Other ingredients, such as peach syrup and cloves, are added.

Cassava leaf soup is produced from cassava leaves, palm oil, chicken bouillon cubes, fresh meat, onion, dry meat, dried fish, pepper, and palm oil. These ingredients combine to produce a tasty soup that goes with rice and other dishes. Its preparation involves boiling ground cassava leaf, ground onion, hot pepper, tomato paste, dry fish, fresh meat, and salt in a pot of water until the water dries up. Palm oil is then added and the compound is stirred for less than 15 minutes before the soup is served. Eggplant stew, made of eggplant, oil, onion, ham or bacon, whitefish fillets, and pepper is also a Liberian delicacy. Palm butter served with white rice is prepared from the residue of the oil palm. Boiled palm nut skins are beaten to pulp to extract oil, which is cooked with crabs, hot peppers, onions, chicken, shrimp or crayfish, and salt. Chicken peanut soup is made from chicken pieces, water, salt, butter, tomato concentrate, black pepper, sliced potato, chopped parsley, and peanut butter. The ingredients are cooked for one hour and served hot. Beans gravy soup is another Liberian culinary delight. It is prepared by soaking a quantity of beans overnight and then boiling it. Half of it is pulverized into pulp, but both the mashed and unmashed beans are later added to a pot of oil, onions, tomato paste, salt, pepper, chicken cubes, and red pepper, all of which are boiled in water until the collection thickens and is ready for consumption with rice.

Goat soup is a national delicacy that is served even at state functions. This culinary practice is shared with other West African peoples, such as the Nigerians to the east. It is a mark of good taste and the height of hospitality in Liberia to slaughter a goat for one's guests. Goat soup is eaten with *foofoo*. Such a meal is taken with palm wine or ginger beer. It is worth noting that though urban and Westernized Liberians eat with cutlery, in most indigenous Liberian homes meals are generally eaten with the fingers, as in other parts of West Africa.

Cakes, Bread, and Pastries

Cakes of various descriptions and provenance (local, foreign, and hybrid) also feature in the diet. One such example is Liberian sweet potato pone, which is made from grated raw sweet potatoes, molasses or dark cane syrup, pulverized ginger, salt, baking powder, and vegetable oil. The ingredients are baked, cut into squares, and served cold or hot. Liberian cake is made of a rich assortment of ingredients: plain flour, baking powder, butter, eggs, sugar, cinnamon, ground mace, milk, lemon peel, raisin (minus the seed), golden syrup, ground allspice, caster sugar, pulverized coconut, and powdered cloves.

These ingredients are baked for a little over half an hour to produce the perfect cake. Cassava cake is produced from an amalgam of cassava, eggs, butter, nutmeg, cinnamon, flour, canned milk, baking powder, cloves, and sugar. These ingredients are mixed with soft residue of peeled cassava that has been pulverized and drained for a few hours and baked for about an hour before it is eaten.

Liberians also eat a variety of breads, including pineapple nut bread and rice bread. Pineapple nut bread is made of flour, baking soda, salt, baking powder, eggs, wheat bran, chopped peanuts or walnuts, and crushed and drained pineapple. These ingredients are baked for one hour to make a unique food item. Ingredients for making rice bread include rice, vegetable oil, nutmeg, mashed bananas, salt, baking oil, and water. Rice bread can last for a week if well made and can serve as either bread or coffee cake.

Cassava and Rice-Based Staples, Vegetables, Oils, and Fruits

Liberian cuisine comprises a variety of main dishes, desserts or appetizers, and soups, ingredients for which include palm oil, pepper, ginger, tomatoes, a variety of vegetables, sweet potatoes, and cassava. However, in spite of this rich assortment, rice remains the main staple of the vast majority of Liberians. The average Liberian rarely goes through a day without a meal of rice. Rice is not eaten without a complement of stew or meat. As in other parts of West Africa, the dish is prepared in various ways. One of the most popular is *jollof* rice, a popular dish across the subregion. Liberian *jollof* rice is a rich amalgam of white rice, pork, bacon, pieces of chicken, veal, turkey, ham, and other condiments. Various types of cooked meat—chicken, shrimp, smoked pork, and bacon—are cut into pieces and compounded with vegetable oil, green peppers, yellow onions, tomatoes, thyme, crushed red pepper, salt, and ground ginger. The result is a delicious delicacy that is relished by children and persons of different classes. It is commonly served at social functions and ceremonies where a large number of guests have to be entertained.

Cassava is the staple of indigenous Liberians, such as the Kpelle, and it is next in importance to rice. Its leaves are eaten as vegetables while the starchy roots or tubers, which can stay in the ground for two years without rotting, substitute for rice when the latter becomes scarce. Rice is often scarce during the rainy season, causing seasonal hunger in varying degrees. However, cassava is processed by grating or pulverization and is fermented to get rid of its prussic acid content before it can be eaten. It is therefore not eaten raw. Processed cassava is fried and boiled before being eaten.

The Liberian diet is enriched by an assortment of fruits and vegetables—peppers, pumpkins, eggplants, okra, beans, tomatoes, onions, mangoes, bananas, pineapples, corn, avocados, cucumbers, and papayas. Palm oil is a major staple of the traditional diet, though it is complemented by imported vegetable oils. Palm oil contains saturated fats, which are potentially detrimental to health, but it is also rich in vitamins. It is extracted from the fruit of the oil palm tree, which grows wild in the forest. The harvested fruits are washed, boiled, and pounded to remove the oil-laden pulp. The pulp is further boiled to extract the oil, which floats on the surface of the water in the container. The oil is separated from the watery residue while the kernels are cracked and further processed to extract a different type of oil from the seed inside the kernel shells. Peanuts feature in many Liberian desserts and cookies. Fried plantain is a favored accompaniment to Liberian rice dishes, or it can be eaten on its own. This delicacy, also popular in other parts of West Africa, is made by slicing several fingers of plantain into thin pieces and frying them in hot oil.

Beverages and Snacks

Ginger beer is a major beverage in Liberia. It is produced from fresh ginger, fresh pineapple, yeast, and molasses. A blend of these items is fermented overnight and seasoned with molasses before it is further diluted with water, ginger, or extra sugar and then consumed. Cane juice, extracted from sugar cane, often with an alcoholic content of over 80 percent, is a potent beverage taken by Liberians, especially in rural areas. Nonalcoholic beverages, such as the ubiquitous Coca-Cola, are retailed all over the country. Billboards advertising such products are displayed prominently at strategic locations, and the soft drinks are retailed by hawkers or proprietors of small roadside kiosks set up for that purpose.

Snacks are an important feature of the Liberian diet. Kanyah or Kanya is a delicious snack produced from rice, sugar, and peanuts. Decorticated peanuts are skinned and roasted, broken into small pieces, and compounded and cooked with other ingredients. The resulting paste is formed into appropriate shapes and eaten. Plantain chips also belong in this category. These are slices of plantain deep-fried in oil to a dark brown color, sprinkled with salt, and eaten. Nontraditional snacks produced by frying a mixture of baking flour, sugar, and butter in vegetable oil are also retailed in the urban centers to meet the requirements of a more sophisticated clientele.

DRESS

Dress Styles and Their Significance

Like cuisine, Liberian dress is a reflection of the multiethnic character of the country as well as the interaction of indigenous and foreign influences.

Religion (see chapter 2) also affects or dictates dress styles, as may be seen in the differences between the attires of the Muslim Mandingo and the Christian Americo-Liberians. In the heyday of their ascendancy, Americo-Liberians adopted Western dress styles, notably three-piece suits, ties, and collars. Indeed, they wore top hats and tailcoats to formal occasions down to the era of President Tubman (1944–71), who, unlike his less formal successor, himself exemplified that trend in dress. The Americo-Liberians were proud of the sartorial style that identified them as civilized as contrasted with the tribal people or country people of the Liberian hinterland. It did not matter that the weather made the wearing of such dress in humid weather an avoidable ordeal. Until the violent change of government in 1980, it was considered uncivilized to appear in public or at government functions in indigenous attire. Western-educated women who wore such dresses were mocked as *lappalonians*—a slur from *lappa* (wrapper), associated with country women.

However, Liberians now dress less formally than in the days of Tubman. William Tolbert, Tubman's successor, set the pace for the informal dress code when he was sworn in as president wearing the safari suit that he had on while racing in from the countryside to fill the constitutional vacuum created by his predecessor's death. He unwittingly began a dress fad that privileged the safari suit with its short sleeves—a style that in any case is more conducive to the sweltering climate. Men still wear Western suits on formal occasions, but the safari suit is decidedly popular.

Liberian men also wear indigenous flowing gowns like their counterparts in neighboring West African countries. The gowns are a by-product of the indigenous weaving industry that, as has been examined in chapter 4, produces country cloth of various types. Locally grown cotton is spun and woven on looms into strips of cloth some four to five inches wide and as long as 50 feet. The strips are sewn together into gowns for men and *lappa* for women. The dominant color of the cloth is white, but dyeing the material in indigo changes it to a darker hue. The Mandingo, Vai, Kissi, Bandi, and Gola are especially adept at producing such country cloth, which is worn by graduates of the Poro schools.

The flowing gowns are richly embroidered with different designs. In common with designs across West Africa, the big gowns are wide enough to stretch from wrist to wrist so that they can be folded over to hang on the shoulders. The embroidery is therefore concentrated on the chest area, which is not covered by the folds, and on the middle of the back just below the neck. Different motifs are represented in the designs; the triangle jutting out in front of the neck can represent a sword, while different animals are also pictured in the embroidery. The flowing gown is popularly known as the Mandingo gown. It is closely associated with Islam, especially if the handwoven cap is donned on top of it, though it has been copied by others who are not necessarily Muslim. Beyond that identification, Liberian Muslim men dress in the fashion of their co-religionists in the Middle East, with shawls around the neck and a perforated skull cap on the head for those who have undertaken the pilgrimage to Mecca and Medina. The distinctive dress of an Alhadj (one who has been to Mecca) confers respect within and outside the Muslim community. Muslim women too have their distinctive mode of dress that conforms to religious standards. They wear a blouse to cover the upper part of the body and tie a wrapper (often two at a time) around the waist. Muslim women customarily wear a shawl around the neck and on top of the head to cover the head, neck, and ears. The dominant color of dress worn by Muslim men and women is white.

Like their counterparts in other West African countries, Liberian women attire themselves in Western and African dress. The more traditional women dress in indigenous blouses and wrappers (*lappa*), whereas younger women and girls wear long skirts and wrap scarves or bandannas around their heads. The *lappa* is often associated with illiterate or less-educated women who are either petty traders or peasant farmers or are, in any case, married. Yet in indigenous Liberian societies, tying the *lappa* around the torso was considered quite significant. It was "a sacred and prayerful beginning to a new day" for women, who considered the act as symbolizing the encircling of the living and dead members of their immediate and extended family, a statement of the continuity of life.[3] More sophisticated women and girls (called the civilized) prefer Western dress. Tie-dyed clothes, which are common in West Africa, are sewn into various types of casual dresses, such as the *boubou,* a loose dress shaped like a woman's nightgown. Although there are Liberian designs, some of these dresses originated in the West or in the neighboring French and British colonies such as Senegal, Côte d'Ivoire, Sierra Leone, Ghana, and Nigeria.

The demand for locally designed clothing has generated a local garment-making industry consisting of tailoring and embroidery. Each of these has its complement of master artisans and seamstresses and their apprentices. Skillful and successful weavers also engage in sewing and embroidery, the men being commissioned to decorate gowns, pillows, bedspreads, tablecloths, and window blinds. Among the Gola, the tailor (known as *yun yai ene,* the one who sews things) has emerged as a specialist in working European textiles into local wares. Tailors who learned their trade in Monrovia or some other urban center are found all over the country with their own apprentices. They operate sewing machines of foreign manufacture to sew material of local and foreign make. Apart from taking orders from their customers, they also make custom clothing for sale to men and women. Men's and women's clothes are richly adorned with embroidery, an art perfected by specialists whose skills are ancillary to those of the garment makers. They too have their own apprenticeship system and constitute an artisanal group in their own right. Embroiderers are significant for finishing up the work of tailors, whose sewn garments are incomplete without the embellishment provided by embroiderers.

Globalization has affected the dress styles of Liberians, especially urban youth. Like their counterparts in other parts of the world, Liberian youth have evolved a distinctive dress style, patterned after the Western mold. Students of tertiary institutions in particular and urban youth in general are casually dressed in baseball caps, jeans, and T-shirts. Formal dress (both Western and indigenous) is worn by this group of Liberians only on special occasions, such as college graduations, job interviews, weddings, and funerals. The prolonged civil war and the consequent economic crisis combined to impoverish the peoples of Liberia. Hence, youth and many other urban dwellers opt for secondhand clothing, especially jeans, trousers, skirts, and shirts. These are attractive not only because of the (comparatively low) cost, but also because they are durable, adaptable, and informal. They do not need regular laundering, and, where this is done, the clothes do not have to be ironed before being worn. In Liberia, as elsewhere in Africa, demand has generated an insatiable demand for, and a boom in the trade of, imported secondhand clothes. Open-air stalls for the sale of used clothes are located in major commercial areas of urban centers and are patronized by men and women of different classes, incomes, and ages.

In addition to clothing, Liberians adorn themselves with complementary items such as necklaces of various types and materials, rings, and bracelets. As indicated in chapter 4, brass jewelry was a popular fashion item up to the late 1930s, when the Liberian government prohibited it. Nonetheless, Liberian men and women still wear ornaments of brass, gold, and silver, depending on their economic or social status. For both traditional and modern women, formal dress is incomplete without these accompaniments. Various types of shoes and slippers are worn by people according to their economic station in life and social status. The shoes are of foreign or local manufacture, the latter including ornate sandals made by the Mandingo.

Hairstyling

The dressing or adornment of the hair is a crucial accompaniment of dress. Consequently, the hair on the head is accorded special attention, obviously because it provides the first impression about an individual. Hence, the hairstyle of a traditional healer or warrior (often adorned with locks or amulets) is necessarily different from that of ordinary persons. An insane person is also identified by his or her unkempt appearance. However, the hair on the head has added importance in African societies because of the supposed ritual and spiritual significance of the human head on which the hair sits. Ordinarily, hairdressing is a mundane task, but in Africa it is a task that has much social and spiritual significance. First, the condition of the hair conveys meanings: grey hair connotes old age that demands respect. Hence, it is a privilege to be asked to assist an older woman in styling her hair. In certain settings, however, people dye their hair to make it black, a hair color that supposedly signifies youth and vitality. Second, hairstyling among women provides the atmosphere for intimate conversation and gossip, and for sharing new ideas. Third, and consequently, people normally choose their hairstylist with care. Such a person must be a close relative or friend, or a friendly neighbor, but never an enemy or a suspected witch. It is commonly believed that an enemy could pick off strands of one's hair for potent magic that could kill the owner or make him or her insane.

Liberian women, like their counterparts in other parts of Africa, tend to cover their heads with scarves of local and foreign manufacture. When a woman is dressed in African prints, the head covering is made of the same material as the wrapper (*lappa*). Among the Mende and other Liberian peoples, women's hair is expected to be dark (black), as brown hair denotes dirtiness. Hence, the hair is washed, well groomed, and plaited in such a way as to attract complimentary comments from other persons, including the woman's spouse. Conversely, disheveled hair is a sign of distress, bereavement, or even insanity. Consequently, special care is taken to make the hair flourish so that it can be easily styled in an attractive way. Hair plaiting by women provides a forum for social bonding and is a sign of the individual's harmony with the larger society.

Hairstyles depict status and power in Liberian societies. Elaborate hairstyles are worn by women of high status who have much time for leisure, such as the wives of chiefs, and they are generally made for ceremonial occasions. Such styles demand patience and sacrifice of time to arrange, and older women tend to opt for less demanding but less glamorous hairstyles. However, younger women, even in the cities, now patronize professional hairstylists to have their hair plaited in the more elaborate styles. They endure the hours of strain required to sit while so many braids are made, as well as the pain produced by the tight pulling of the hair, to make themselves more appealing to prospective suitors. The hairstylists vary their designs to give some uniqueness to the end product of their endeavors.

Hairstyling is of various types: plaiting, braiding, twisting, and reverse braiding. While plaiting and twisting involve the use of special threads, braiding does not require anything other than the women's hair itself. However, in recent times, urban women in particular have been adding artificial hair to their braids to make them longer. The addition of artificial hair is a foil for short hair, but it indicates that long hair is considered an index of beauty. The increasing preference for long hair—and the pains taken to artificially elongate it—is also suggestive of the imitation of the hair of women of other races. Hairstyles on indigenous masks carved in the nineteenth and early twentieth centuries give an idea of hairstyles that have become extinct. The one on the *sowei* mask of the Vai and Mende is the high-ridged type that is now considered old-fashioned among many Liberian peoples today. In some areas, though, the high-ridged hairstyle was modified to a low-ridged type, which was worn by Mende women as late as the 1980s. This hairstyle consisted of parallel ridges of hair of equal height that covered all parts of the head as opposed to the older type that covered the ridge of the head only. Raffia and other objects are also braided into the hair to enhance its length the way artificial hair is attached to many modern women's hair.

Traditional coiffure has both aesthetic and spiritual significance among the Gola, Vai, Mende, Bassa, Loma, and Bandi, especially in the context of initiation of young girls into Sande. In earlier times, girls went into or returned from the Sande bush school with elaborately coiffured hair. They underwent the combing of the hair ceremony, a public styling of their hair in the company of their friends and relatives. On their graduation, their hair was done in different styles according to regional traditions. Among the Bassa, Gola, Mende, and Vai, the hair was bunched up to reveal the forehead, but in the Loma and Bandi areas, the hair was styled to hang down the young women's faces. Apart from the symbolism of their initiation, the hairstyles were meant to make the women attractive to suitors since they were now ready for marriage.

The traditional hairstyle for Liberian men was generally uniform; the hair was closely cropped as depicted on the extant masks and other carvings. However, men's hair was braided when they graduated from the Poro school and when they were due for burial. Men in Dan society traditionally wore a hairstyle characterized by a round patch of hair on the forehead and the sides of the head shaved, leaving a luxuriant growth on the ridge of the head, or a number of thick locks surrounded by shaved portions. Soothsayers' hair was styled with dots of shaved spots, with bells attached for effect. The influence of globalization on Liberian men and women's hairstyles is best seen in the urban centers, where a great variety of hairstyles are on display. As in dress style, many youth copy the hairstyles of famous sports stars, musicians, and actors in Africa and the West.

NOTES

1. Syrulwa Somah, "Promoting Agricultural Production in the New Liberia," http://www.ie-inc.com/vkarmo/Articles/Somak_Agro.pdf, accessed June 15, 2005.
2. Esther Warner Dendel, *African Fabric Crafts: Sources of African Design and Technique* (New York: Taplinger, 1974), p. 148.
3. Ibid.

REFERENCES

Arnoldi, Mary Jo, and Christine Kreamer Mueller. *Crowning Achievements: African Arts of Dressing the Head.* Los Angeles: University of California and Fowler Museum of Cultural History, 1995.
Boone, Sylvia Ardyn. *Radiance from the Waters: Ideals of Feminine Beauty in Mende Art.* New Haven, Conn.: Yale University Press, 1986.
Bruyninx, Elze. "Coiffures of the Dan and We in Ivory Coast in 1938–1939." In *Hair in African Art and Culture,* ed. Roy Sieber and Frank Herremann. Munich: Prestel Books, 2000, pp. 79–84.
Conteh, Al-Hassan. "Reflections on Some Concepts of Religion and Medicine in Liberian Society," *Liberian Studies Journal* 15, no. 2 (1990): 145–57.
Dendel, Esther Warner. *African Fabric Crafts: Sources of African Design and Technique.* New York: Taplinger, 1974.
Lamb, Venice, and Alastair Lamb. *Sierra Leone Weaving.* Hertingfordbury, United Kingdom: Roxford Books, 1984.
"Liberian Cuisine," LiberianForum.Com, http://www.liberianforum.com/recipe.htm, accessed June 15, 2005.
Martin, Phillip. "African Recipes," http://www.phillipmartin.info/liberia/text_recipes_intro.htm, accessed June 15, 2005.
Sandler, Bea. *The African Cookbook.* New York: Carol, 1993.
Sieber, Roy, and Frank Herreman (eds.). *Hair in African Art and Culture.* Munich: Prestel Books, 2000.
Siegmann, William. "Women's Hair and Sowei Masks in Southern Sierra Leone and Western Liberia." In *Hair in African Art and Culture,* ed. Roy Sieber and Frank Herremann. Munich: Prestel Books, 2000, pp. 71–78.
Somah, Syrulwa. "Promoting Agricultural Production in the New Liberia," http://www.ie-inc.com/vkarmo/Articles/Somak_Agro.pdf, accessed June 15, 2005.
Wilson, Ellen. *A West African Cookbook.* New York: Evans, 1971.

6

Gender Roles, Marriage, and Family

Women are socialized ... to be more conservative than men in their occupational aspirations and often depend on marriage for their social status.
>—Janice M. Saunders, educational theorist[1]

In Kpelle society, men are considered to be superior to women physically, intellectually, and morally. Women are legally subordinate to men.
>—Soniia David, sociologist[2]

The Glebo have inserted gender into the civilized/native dichotomy to the point where women's status is not only more tenuous and vulnerable than men's but also very difficult to maintain without male support.
>—Mary H. Moran, anthropologist[3]

THIS CHAPTER EXAMINES the interlocking issues of gender roles, marriage, and family. It highlights traditional and modern practices and the changes wrought by Christianity and Western literacy. As in other chapters of this book, a rough distinction is drawn between traditional and modern practices, between the hinterland peoples and the coastal settler community. Even so, it is clear that such distinctions are no longer valid in some cases given extensive interactions and intermarriage across the various divides. It is important, however, to highlight the various differences in marriage and family practices and gender roles given the strength of traditional practices that have ensured the maintenance of certain distinctiveness among the various peoples of Liberia. It also permits an understanding of what has changed and what remains. While it may not be possible to give the specific characteristics of the various ethnic groups in Liberia, it may be necessary to illustrate some points with specific examples. Note, however, that many of the traditional practices have been eroded from the 1960s onward.

TRADITIONAL MARRIAGE IN LIBERIAN COMMUNITIES

The institution of marriage in indigenous African societies stood at the intersection of gender roles and family life. Especially for male members, marriage in such societies was an index of maturity and an emblem of citizenship in the local community. In all these spheres, the various African peoples had a clear understanding of the rights and obligations of constituent members of the family, lineage, or community and of the parties to a marriage. Undoubtedly, marriage was never simply a contract between the couple; rather, it was a bond between the couple and their respective in-laws and kinsfolk. The general pattern in a patrilineal society was that marriage involved the transfer or exchange of individual and property rights. The family of the husband was entitled to the woman's domestic and other conjugal services, her other assets, and the products of the union. In exchange, her family was entitled to the bridewealth in kind or in cash payable by the groom and his family. The product of such unions belonged to the husband and his patrilineal family, hence the Vai saying *kai wa tamu deng nda*—a child belongs to his father.[4]

As in most other African societies, male suitors were expected to pay bridewealth in cash or in kind (e.g., supply of labor and sundry service to the wife's family) in return for which the wife discharged certain obligations. After the marriage had been fully consummated, the wife was expected to bear and rear children for her husband; work on the farm to produce (and prepare) food for the household; assist her husband in maintaining his parents; respect or defer to her in-laws; and earn income for the family through various commercial activities such as the marketing of palm oil, rice, and vegetables.

Traditional marriage practice and family structure in Liberia permitted polygyny and its variants. Yet differences existed in the marriage practices of the various indigenous groups during the premodern era. Some communities, such as the Kpelle and Grebo, permitted the practice of levirate, by which a widow was expected to marry a kin of her deceased spouse. Among the Grebo, a son could inherit his father's wives (except his own mother, of course) while a nephew could inherit his uncle's wives. This was because a woman and her children were deemed to belong to the lineage that paid the bridewealth to her family. Furthermore, in the event of a divorce, a woman and her family were required to refund the bridewealth paid on her. The Gbandi practiced both levirate and sororate marriages.[5] However, though it was permitted, levirate was seldom practiced by the Kpelle. Among several Liberian peoples, some marriage practices were forbidden. The Grebo forbade sororate marriage while the Krahn prohibited marriage between members of the same clan. The Belle prohibited marriage to the wives of the maternal uncle. This contrasted with the Gola practice that permitted first cousin and sororate marriages. Beyond formal marriage, less-formal relationships were also recognized by society. However, men had no legal rights to the products of cohabitation in an informal relationship.

The procedure for betrothal and marriage among the Bassa followed an established pattern. First came the contact phase (*kmohn bein*), when the prospective suitor formally informed his parents that he had seen a girl that he wanted to "catch." If his parents approved of the girl and her family (the latter had to have a good reputation in the community), they would consent to the next step, known as touch[ing] the shoulder (*bah-sohn-kohn*). With her family duly informed, the suitor could make a direct proposal to the girl and, at this stage, he had marked her as his so that no other suitor was permitted to have any liaison with her. She was deemed to be engaged to the suitor. The third stage, known as *khna-gbo whon-hwie* or closing the door, committed him to her family. This commitment implied the male's willingness to shoulder whatever responsibilities accompanied his marriage. Finally, having secured the consent of the bride's parents, the *nynohn-dohnon* (literally, purchasing the woman) took place with the presentation of the *po-bui* (trust fund), which included money, food, domestic animals, and cloth to the bride's parents, who determined what must be delivered by the suitor's family. The payment of what amounts to the bridewealth could involve the supply of labor. The groom's parents generally assisted their son in fulfilling his obligations.

It can be deduced that, among the Bassa, the traditional marriage system involved the payment of bride-price, known locally as dowry, or bride service of 7 to 10 years. Second, there had to be evidence of the couple's ability to be self-supporting. Third, the couple married out of personal choice and also determined where to live—with either partner's parents—after marriage. Men could not lay claim to their children until they had fully discharged all their obligations to their spouse's family. Widows also determined whether to stay with their late husband's kin or go elsewhere, such as to their natal family.

Among the Kpelle, marriage was regarded as a process or a series of stages beginning from a girl's initiation into Sande and proceeding through betrothal, coresidence, the payment of the bridewealth to seal the union, and, finally, to the arrival of the first one or two issues in the relationship. The payment of bridewealth, called the turning over of the woman to the man, was a critical point in the process. It took place at the bride's family house and was witnessed by her kin and those of her spouse, with both partners in attendance. The turning over was symbolic in that the amount involved was a mere token.

The event was normally devoid of elaborate ceremony or festivity. The betrothal of a Kpelle woman was done in her childhood by her parents, but the turning over did not take place until she had attained puberty. Male Kpelle also needed parental consent, which was given when he was considered capable of starting a rice farm. In some cases, young suitors could bypass parental consent if the girl had not been betrothed in childhood.

The Belle traditional system of marriage was similar in some respects to systems of other Liberian groups. Betrothal started with the approach by a young man to his prospective wife, to whom he gave a ring. On showing the ring to her parents, she was asked her opinion of the proposal, and if she was agreeable, her parents gave their consent. The young man's parents then made a formal approach to their son's parents-in-law by presenting a package of salt to them. Salt symbolized the supplication, joy (sweetness), peace, noble intentions, and sincerity that are expected to pervade or characterize the proposal and consummation of marriage . The woman's parents registered their consent by accepting the present, after which the bride-price was paid. Payment was made in kind, with a cow and a slave or a bundle of iron. This finally consummated the marriage, after which the wife moved in with her husband. The Belle had taboos that forbade sexual relations between a man and his maternal uncle's wives, but he could marry any of his maternal cousins. Ancient tradition permitted a man to have intimate relations with two sisters provided he started with the elder sister. Otherwise, he was forbidden access to the elder sister, who was regarded as his sister-in-law if he was already cohabiting with the younger woman.

Yet women were strictly forbidden from keeping multiple partners at the same time. If any woman committed such an act, a Poro masked dancer lampooned her in public for causing disaffection between two men and imposed a penalty on her in the form of feasting all the men in the community with rice. The woman was also compelled to make a choice between the two men; the chosen one was publicly proclaimed while the loser was directed to desist from any further liaison with her. Defaulters were liable to a severe retribution. This practice was to forestall disaffection that could rupture the fabric of an essentially communal society. Social control of this type by the Poro was meant to promote social harmony, even if at the expense of an individual's free choice.

Polygyny was central to indigenous marriage systems given the prevailing cultural norms by which men measured or advanced their political and economic fortunes by the number of their wives. Paradoxically, the first wife played a role in the acquisition of other wives by recruiting them for her husband as junior wives, who were in practical terms their household help. If a husband needed another wife, the senior wife would look for a woman with whom she maintained cordial relations. Conversely, if her husband expressed interest in a girl she did not like, she turned the situation to her own advantage by getting a divorce. This suggests that, in spite of the patriarchal nature of the indigenous societies of Liberia, women still retained a certain measure of autonomy in the decision to remain in or get out of marriage relationships. Even where relatives mediated in domestic disputes, the decision to dissolve or sustain the marriage was left entirely to the couple, especially the wife. A woman could contrive a divorce by picking a quarrel over her husband's choice of a junior wife by accusing him of neglect or favoritism or of physical assault. She could provoke him to beat her, which amounted to maltreatment, considered grounds for divorce, by refusing to perform her domestic or conjugal duties. The husband too could file for divorce on the grounds of the wife's infidelity.

For whatever reasons it was granted, divorce necessitated the sharing of assets on the basis of some established principles: the partner who was responsible for the divorce got less than his or her partner; property was awarded to the partner who earned a cash income (usually the man); if the woman had custody of the children, she was awarded tangible assets like houses and rice farms even if she was adjudged guilty of adultery. The situation was different if formal marriage was not consummated. In the event of a breakup, each party in a relationship of cohabitation went away with their individual assets. Products of those unions usually belonged to the woman's family since the children's biological father had not fulfilled his obligations to her family. The Kpelle had various types of trial marriages: long-term relationships; clandestine affairs; and freelancing, where women maintained sexual liaisons with several partners concurrently. Cohabitation and trial marriages reveal the permissiveness of Kpelle society with regard to premarital sex. The offspring of such affairs belonged to their mother's family unless their father(s) opted to underwrite the woman's pre- and postnatal expenses.

Traditional marriage in Liberia served more than the purpose of procreation or raising families; it was also an economic venture. Wives supported their husband directly by generating income or supplying labor at home and on the farms. Marriage also enabled a big man (a wealthy and influential man) to increase his following as people gave him their daughters, whom he would marry as junior or lower-status wives but whom he might permit to engage in liaisons with young men and male clients so that the latter could be made to pay for such cohabitation by working on the big man's farms. This was in keeping with the custom that husbands were entitled to damages for adultery committed by their wives, even where this had been contrived by the husband with the wife's complicity. Such big men also employed their marital ties to build alliances with neighboring communities for commercial and political advantages. Marriage likewise served the purpose of integrating stranger elements into a host community. As indicated in chapter 2, the Mandingo employed this strategy to integrate themselves into the societies of the Kpelle and Vai. They married indigenous women both to facilitate their indigenization and to spread their religion of Islam. However, to preserve their religious and social identity in the host community, the Mandingo never gave out their own daughters to the local people. Marriage alliances were also employed to forge mythical relationships between autochthonous communities and later arrivals. A land-owning lineage would offer a daughter to the strangers, who then adopted the donor-lineage as an uncle. Such an uncle-nephew relationship existed between the Loma and the Kissi. Among the Loma, the wife-giving lineages were called *keke* and the receivers were known as *daaba*.

Contrary to the impression that the foregoing applied to all males in the community, it is worth stressing that there were actually different classes of husbands in Kpelle society at least. In one category were men who were clients of big men patrons or strangers, including fugitives from other places, who could not get any relatives or local surrogate father to lend them the bride-wealth or stand surety for the marriage. Such so-called wife borrowers became beholden to their patrons for as long as they were unable to pay their bride-wealth themselves, and they often ended up completely integrated into their patron's families. Their new identities were then legitimized through the creation of fictional genealogies linking them to the patron's lineage. If the wife borrowers managed to offset their debts, they made the transition to wife keepers. But this was after they had fully settled debts relating not only to bride-wealth but also to sundry claims like taxes, school fees, clothing, and medical care. The big man or wife lender, to whom the other two types of husbands were beholden, profited from the arrangement, especially if he had gotten the women in question betrothed to him either before or after they were born. He would commit resources to the prospective bride's family by giving gifts to her parents or supporting her materially in other ways. If, however, the girl grew up to renege on the childhood betrothal agreement, her preferred spouse would either fully reimburse the big man or become his client.

Another marriage practice among the Kpelle, also prevalent elsewhere, was cross-cousin marriage, which took place between direct children or descendants of siblings of the opposite sex. In most cases, it involved a man and the daughter of his female cousin. Such marriages were often problematic in that the wife could defy the husband with impunity since their co-relatives would step in to prevent him from assaulting her. Hence, men who were eligible to marry their cousin's daughters preferred to transfer their rights to a dependent young man, who was thus put in their debt. Cousin marriage was, therefore, another means of building up networks of patron-client relationships.

Indigenous marriage took various forms, but most parents preferred an endogamous arrangement that allowed their children, especially the daughters, to remain in the locality with their spouses and family. This would enable them to continue to harness the labor of their children and their families. Stories were told of the danger in marrying handsome strangers who might be monsters or evil spirits in disguise to discourage daughters from marrying, and eventually leaving with, strangers. Although brides were not for sale, parents stood to gain from bridewealth, the labor of their sons-in-law, and the benefits of marital ties to a big man. Such considerations weighed significantly in the determination of their children's choice of partner. Each of the choices had implications for the parties to the marriage—older suitors would offer bridewealth but would not be able to offer bride service; the reverse was the case for struggling young men; and big men would offer neither bridewealth nor service but would dispense occasional favors, which fell short of the parents' aspirations.

Bridewealth paid in cash, cloth, kola nuts and goats was generally beyond the means of the average young suitor. But he could struggle to pay it himself, draw on the resources of his family (as a loan), or become the client of a big man for that purpose. If he could pay the bridewealth, he was ordinarily spared the demands of his parents-in-law for bride service. Yet bridewealth was not seen as a one-off payment; no matter what the husband had given, he was still expected to make payments in cash or in kind as long as the marriage subsisted. Hence, he was expected to contribute to the funeral expenses of his in-laws. Those who paid their bridewealth with the aid of their relatives were thereby indebted to their kinsfolk, who might occasionally refer to it to keep them in check. The point is that traditional marriages constituted a web of dependent relationships. Young men who were at the receiving end could maneuver by paying their bridewealth with the aid of their kin and by moving away from their in-laws to live a more independent life. However, in northwestern Liberian communities, the tradition of cousin marriage permitted a young man to avoid paying bridewealth. No payments were required if such a person married his maternal cousin, the daughter of his mother's brother, or, at any rate, a member of his mother's lineage.

MODERNITY AND MARRIAGE

Generally in Liberia, traditional marriage laws permit a man to contract as many as three or four marriages and cohabit with all the women at the same time. All that is required is the payment of the bridewealth or dowry, which includes cash payment. In spite of the inherent problems in the arrangement, traditional marriage is expected to last till death or divorce separate the partners.

Conversely, statutory marriage, the product of the influence of Western culture, is based on monogamy, which subsists until death or divorce terminates the relationship. Such marriages follow prescribed standards, such as the procurement of statutory health and marriage certification. They are consummated by an officiating cleric, judicial official, or captain of a Liberian-registered vessel. Any breach of the regulations prescribing monogamy, such as a concurrent statutory marriage to another person, amounts to bigamy, which attracts judicial sanctions. Any other concurrent union is regarded in law as a nullity. In effect, Liberian marriage laws do not permit a concurrent marriage (whether traditional or statutory) to a third party by any party to a statutory marriage. In practice, however, this law is observed in the breach, particularly by powerful individuals such as leading political figures and other members of the ruling class.

Privileged members of Liberian society, including the self-professed Christians and those who had contracted elaborate civilized marriages, have resorted to keeping mistresses or concubines, with whom they had children. Other less privileged men have also maintained a façade of monogamy while practicing polygyny. They keep the so-called civilized wives in the city and even live in the same house with them and their children while maintaining another wife, often a country woman in the village. This is not peculiar to Liberians but is a widespread practice by many literate, generally Christian, men along the West African coast.

Today, the two systems of marriage coexist with the statutory marriages being privileged compared to the traditional. Widows under the statutory arrangement inherit their husband's property, whereas their counterparts are treated as chattel to be inherited with the physical possessions of their husbands. Given that the woman married under customary law is treated as property, she cannot ordinarily inherit her husband's property. Such disability is compounded by the fact that under the Liberian constitution, all matters pertaining to customary law are treated administratively with the president being the final arbiter. Hence, the women married under this arrangement are at the mercy of a system that is not subject to due process of the formal law courts. Statutory marriage, in contrast, is covered by the law, and aggrieved parties can pursue their claims right up to the supreme court.

Marriage practices in Liberia have been shaped by the factors of indigenous culture and external influences including Islam, Christianity, and Western education. In terms of family structure, Christianity rather than Islam has had a more profound effect. First, Islam, unlike Christianity, does not prohibit polygyny and is more tolerant of indigenous practices like levirate. Second, Christianity and formal education make Liberians more prone to living in nuclear families, whereas Islamic marriages generally produce more offspring and larger families, which are more akin to indigenous African practices.

GENDER AND FAMILY

A feature of the patriarchal social system prevalent in Liberian communities is the dominance of men over women. As the discussion in the previous section has shown in the context of marriage relationships, men were almost always rated above women. An exception were women of great spiritual influence, called *mabole* by the Mende, who were regarded with awe and deference even by men because they were responsible for a critical aspect of the closing ceremonies of the Poro initiation. Such exceptional women were regarded as men and were given custody of the instrument for circumcising male initiates. Nonetheless, many indigenous Liberian patrilineal societies, such as the Kpelle, maintained a gender-based division of labor.

Agricultural work was a group activity in which men undertook the harder tasks such as bush clearing while the women planted the seed. Ancillary activities, such as hunting, harvesting of kola nuts and palm nuts, and tapping the oil palm tree for wine, were male preserves. The menfolk plaited mats, made furniture, and wove indigenous cloth. Women were dominant in other activities, such as fishing and gathering, and net and basket making. Male dominance was hinged on men's monopoly of strategic occupations such as blacksmithing, which had mystical attributes, and on the accumulation of wealth in money, material, and people. Leading members of Poro (for men) and Sande (for women) and traditional medicine men and women enjoyed great prestige, as did the wealthy and influential big men.

Gender relations in the Kpelle agricultural economy were unique in their flexibility in that men and women did not have exclusive control over any crops. This was reflected in the interchange of crops by the sexes, the mutual help (by the man for his wife) in cultivating the household farm in addition to each spouse's personal farms. There were no special crops for men or areas of production that were taboo for women. With the exception of upland and swamp rice, sugarcane, coffee, cocoa, and cassava were planted by either gender. Kpelle society upheld male dominance but acknowledged the wife's responsibility for providing for her family. However, like other Liberian peoples, the Kpelle have been responsive to the pressures of modernity. A study of Kpelle family budgeting showed that most husbands still kept the family purse, and their spouses were generally dependent to that extent.[6] This suggests the resilience of patriarchal attitudes, though women have also developed their own survival strategies.

Man working in a rice field in
a small village (July 2, 1997).
© Mikkel Ostergaard/VISUM/
The Image Works.

A contrasting situation existed among the Grebo (Glebo), a Kruan-speaking people of southeastern Liberia, with regard to gender roles and family life. Though men indeed carried out the most tasking jobs on the farms, such as cutting down and burning big trees at the commencement of the agricultural cycle and erecting fences to protect the rice fields from infestation by pests, their involvement in agricultural work was for a comparatively short section of the cycle. For the rest of the period, women labored in the fields, turning the cleared ground with the hoe, planting the seed, weeding the field, and harvesting and processing the crops. In effect, Grebo women supplied the bulk of the agricultural labor that ensured the success of the region's agricultural economy. They were responsible for interplanting the rice fields with vegetables, cultivating cassava (in addition to rice), and marketing the cash crops. Thus, among the Grebo, the women were ideally the breadwinners, the hardworking farmers who controlled rice production and fed their husbands. The latter were expected in accordance with accepted gender division of labor to secure land for the family through their patrilineages, provide a house for their households, and earn income from wage employment or cash cropping. Yet the peasant or petty trader Grebo wife acknowledged her subordination to her husband and did not even expect him to contribute to the family budget.

The foregoing structure of the average country or native family, however, contrasts with that of the so-called civilized family in Grebo society. While the former functioned on the model of a female breadwinner (responsible for the domestic budget of the household), the civilized family unit consisted of the male breadwinner and the female homemaker. Civilized husbands prided themselves that their wives did not work to earn a living but devoted their time to raising children and sustaining the image of a civilized family. Yet the women were not idle: they engaged themselves in the micro business of making or retailing pancakes, popcorn, and biscuits or in more extensive business enterprises, utilizing motor transport to distribute foodstuffs such as banana, cassava, and plantain. Such efforts, however, are not regarded as employment or an alternative to the supply received from the male breadwinner.

Islam has also influenced gender roles in Liberian communities, such as the Vai, in which the religion plays a dominant role. In the indigenous funerary practice of the Vai, women participated and even officiated in graveside ceremonies and in the communal prayers. But with the coming of Islam, they ceased to perform such functions. They nevertheless continue to pound the rice that is eaten as part of the funerary rites.

Urbanization has shaped gender roles in Liberia in contrast to traditional gender relations described previously. Although the model of a civilized woman is still popular, the realities of urban life ensure that women have to work to support their husbands, even if minimally. However, for most urban women, especially homemakers, life is a daily struggle. This reality can be deduced from Bai T. Moore's poem (cited in chapter 3) that depicts how Monrovia market women get up early every day to take care of themselves and their babies before rushing off to the market. Women among that class strive for (and duly achieve) financial independence in the urban centers by dint of hard work.

Formal education and family circumstances have also affected gender roles and interactions in contemporary Liberia. Although female children are still disadvantaged in many communities, those with access to formal education have been able to assert themselves in the formal sector and in the economy in general. When such young women are able to acquire university degrees or secure gainful employment, their status is further enhanced. Family circumstances help where both parents of a female child are themselves members of the educated elite. As the career of Fatima Massaquoi Fahnbulleh (1912–78), detailed in the next section, epitomizes, a female child with a progressive father like hers could attain any heights in Liberian society.

However, for most Liberian families, the male child is privileged compared to his sisters. The discrimination starts from childhood, when young girls are made to bear the brunt of household chores, assisting their mothers in cooking, fetching water, and running related errands. Girls also look after their younger siblings from an early age, especially when the parents are at work.

Women's Monument on the wall in front of
the Centennial Hall (Monrovia). © Topham/
The Image Works.

Conversely, young boys, who admittedly mature much later than girls, are
freed from the responsibility of most domestic chores and have more time to
devote to their studies or play. As in other West African countries, the extended
family in Liberia can strain itself to pool resources to fund the education of
their male members but hardly ever does so for their daughters. This is because
families anticipate that the (educated) woman will take her assets (bestowed
by her family of orientation) to her husband's family, a development that is
seen as a net loss to the woman's family. Even when children irrespective of
gender are given a chance to study, they are generally channeled into curricula
according to an artificial order of gender capability. That is, boys are routed
into the sciences and mathematics and the girls into supposedly less tasking
courses. Moreover, some professions, such as teaching and nursing, are treated
as female preserves. The implication of this is that girls are given limited
options in education and career development and are therefore programmed
to be less adventurous and more conservative in outlook. In any case, given
the premium placed on marriage, some parents fear that a female child who
is too highly educated might find it more difficult to find a man to marry her
compared to her less educated counterparts. This supposition indicates that
men often feel threatened by women or wives who are more accomplished.

In a general sense, the institution of marriage remains central to daily life in
Liberia, in spite of the trauma of the protracted civil war occasioned by the
high death toll and population movements. Unlike in many Western societies,

Old woman carrying water on her head in a small village (July 2, 1997). © Mikkel Ostergaard/VISUM/The Image Works.

getting married is seen as a symbol of social status. In urban centers like Monrovia, marriage is a sign of responsibility, and a person with a stable home is considered to be highly responsible. Such persons are believed to be capable of holding public office or being saddled with leadership in the society. Moreover, strategic marriage partnerships with wealthy or influential families, as well as membership in secret societies or notable religious organizations (especially churches), have helped aspirants to secure political positions or other pecuniary privileges. This was most prevalent in the pre-1980 era of Americo-Liberian ascendancy, when indigenous Liberians achieved social mobility by marrying into the leading families of the period.

Two concomitants of marriage—procreation and widowhood—represent the intersection of gender, marriage, and family among Liberian peoples. As a general rule, procreation remains central to marriage. The birth of children is celebrated and there are formal ceremonies for the christening of children. It is understood that the children belong not to their parents alone but to the lineage, clan, and the wider society. Consequently, traditional child rearing is a shared responsibility of the parents and other agents of socialization. Single births are the norm, but multiple births or deformed children are viewed with awe. Among the Kpelle, for example, twins (especially identical ones) are given special attention and care. Deformed children were usually killed at birth as they were considered to be spirits (*jinaa*) and, therefore, a threat to the community. Identical twins were likewise viewed with awe and surrounded by superstitions and restrictions. But they were not killed. Both (or one) of identical male twins were believed by the Kpelle to be predestined to be *zonga* (powerful medicine men). Where only one was destined to be, according to indigenous belief, he would betray the trait by his aggressive behavior. That *zo* twin, it was held, might kill his twin brother or father in future. Twins were treated with caution and nobody was permitted to knock them on the head, even accidentally. Identical twins were, however, required to observe certain bush meat taboos, and they were to be given gifts in equal proportion so as not to arouse jealousy that could prove fatal in the future.[7]

While the birth of children is celebrated in Liberian society, the absence of children in marriage inflicts pain on the couple and the wider circle of family and friends. Efforts are made to ascertain the causes (it often being attributed to sorcery by adversaries or malevolent spirits) and remedy the situation by traditional and modern means. If childlessness persists for several years, it generally strains relationships to the point of separation or divorce. The wife is generally held responsible for this, and her in-laws encourage their kinsman to take another wife to produce children for him. Hence, childlessness is a major threat to marriages contracted even by self-professed Christians, who easily yield to pressure from their relatives to contract another marriage or divorce the childless woman. The predicament of the childless wife, who is also expected to take care of her step- or foster children, is highlighted in Bai T. Moore's poem "Ba Nya M Go Koma" (in Liberian Pidgin, "They Said I Did Not Born"). The plight of such women is further aggravated by widowhood, which leaves them at the mercy of unsympathetic in-laws, the most insensitive of whom are often other women. This shows only that, as in other African countries, Liberian women still suffer some culturally determined institutional disadvantages. Only in exceptional cases, as exemplified by Fatima Massaquoi Fahnbulleh, where women are privileged by birth, marriage, or education are these disadvantages substantially remedied.

A Rare Exception: Fatima Massaquoi Fahnbulleh (1912–78)

Fatima Massaquoi, whose father, Momolu Massaquoi (1870–1938), was Liberia's pioneer consul general in Hamburg (1922–29), was admittedly a rare exception even for the contemporary times. Her mother, Madam Massa Balo Sonjo, was from the Barri chiefdom in Sierra Leone, and her father was a member of an aristocratic Vai family, his mother being the formidable Queen Sandimannie. Educated in Liberia, Switzerland, Germany, and the United States and graduating with a bachelor's and two master's degrees from American universities, Fatima was fluent in German, French, English, Italian, Vai, and Mende. Her life had been shaped by the strong personalities of her father and her paternal aunt, Ma Jassa; immersion in her indigenous

Vai culture (being initiated into Sande); and her vast international exposure. Momolu Massaquoi's determination to give his favorite child (and only daughter) the best form of education was to make Fatima the pioneer woman educator in Liberia. She was also a rare exception for a member of the indigenous community in Liberia.

Following her father's unsuccessful bid for the Liberian presidency in 1931 and the collapse of his political and economic fortunes, culminating in his death in 1938, Fatima faced hard times in the United States. Still, she completed her education (though she never submitted her doctoral dissertation) before returning to Liberia in October 1946 on the invitation of President William V. S. Tubman. Appointed professor of French and science at Liberia College in March 1947, Fatima participated in the development of higher education in Liberia, achieving a series of firsts. Before retiring in 1972, she had been the director, then dean, of the College of Liberal and Fine Arts; founding director of the Institute of African Studies, cofounder of the Society of Liberian Authors, and acting president of the University of Liberia for a brief spell in 1958. Her labor earned her an honorary doctorate from the University of Liberia and several local and international honors, including the award of the Grand Star of Africa with the rank of Grand Commander (Liberia), the German Grand Meritorious Cross First Class (Grobe Verdienstrkreuz erster Klasse), and the Tricentenary Bust of Molière (France). In addition to curriculum development, Fatima made notable contributions in the cultural and social development of the university and the country. She successfully led the campaign against the requirement that students wear academic gowns on campus and that they drop their indigenous names for foreign ones. In this connection, she made her husband drop his adopted surname of Freeman for the original one of Fahnbulleh on the eve of their wedding on July 26, 1948. She taught the Vai language in Germany and promoted it at home, to the point of organizing in 1962 a seminar on standardization of the Vai script, a notable landmark in the development of the script.

Fatima Massaquoi Fahnbulleh died on November 26, 1978, a rare Liberian woman, a versatile educator, polyglot, and internationalist who was also a cultural nationalist of note. To be sure, Liberia has also produced other outstanding women, including Mary Antoinette Brown Sherman, the first woman president of the University of Liberia and the first woman to head a university in Africa and Angie Brooks, the country's representative at the United Nations. Liberia has also produced notable women political leaders, such as Ruth Perry, a one-time interim head of state, and President Ellen Johnson-Sirleaf.

Born in Liberia on October 29, 1938 and educated at Harvard University, Ellen Johnson-Sirleaf has had a distinguished career as secretary of state for finance in the Tolbert government (1972–73), finance minister in the Doe

Angie Brooks at the United Nations,
October 30, 1959. Courtesy of the
Library of Congress.

government (1980–85) and, subsequently, as an economist with Citibank
and the World Bank. Her political activism began in earnest under the Doe
regime and she was jailed for her criticism of that government. She subsequently supported Charles Taylor's rebellion against Doe and fled into exile.
Johnson-Sirleaf returned to Liberia to contest against Taylor, having parted
ways with him, in the 1997 presidential elections as the candidate of the
Unity Party. But in that election, she won only 10 percent of the vote. Her
showing improved significantly in the presidential election of October 2005
when she received 175,200 votes behind the front-runner, the soccer legend,
George Weah. A run-off election was held, however, because no clear winner
emerged and Johnson-Sirleaf subsequently won the run-off election with
almost 60 percent of the popular votes. On November 11, 2005, she was
formally declared winner and president-elect of Liberia by the National Elec-
toral Commission. An independent inquiry considered the allegations of
irregularities made by her opponent but affirmed that she had been validly
elected in the run-off. She thus accomplished the major feat of being the first
woman to be elected president of an African country. Ellen Johnson-Sirleaf
has four sons and six grandchildren. She assumes office in January 2006.

NOTES

1. Janice M. Saunders, "Liberian Higher Education at Cuttington University
College: Are Both Sexes Equal?" *Liberian Studies Journal* 16, no. 2 (1991): p. 87.

2. Soniia David, "'You Become One in Marriage': Domestic Budgeting among the Kpelle of Liberia," *Canadian Journal of African Studies* 30, no. 2 (1996): 160.

3. Mary H. Moran, "Woman and 'Civilization': The Intersection of Gender and Prestige in Southeastern Liberia," *Canadian Journal of African Studies* 22, no. 3, special issue: Current Research on African Women (1988): 499.

4. Bai Tamia Moore, "Problems of Vai Identity in Terms of My Own Experience," *Liberian Studies Journal* 15, no. 2 (1990): 12.

5. Levirate was a practice whereby a widow married her deceased husband's brother or kin; sororate was marriage of one man to two or more sisters, usually successively and after the first wife was found to be barren or after her death.

6. David, "'You Become One in Marriage.'"

7. Bush meat refers to game killed by hunters in contrast to domestic animals and poultry.

REFERENCES

Bledsoe, Caroline H. *Women and Marriage in Kpelle Society.* Stanford, Calif.: Stanford University Press, 1980.

David, Soniia. "'You Become One in Marriage': Domestic Budgeting among the Kpelle of Liberia," *Canadian Journal of African Studies* 30, no. 2 (1996): 157–82.

Erchak, Gerald M. "Who Is the Zo? A Study of Kpelle Identical Twins," *Liberian Studies Journal* 7, no. 1 (1975–77): 23–25.

Jackson, Linda. "Sociocultural and Ethnohistorical Influences on Genetic Diversity in Liberia," *American Anthropologist* 88, no. 4 (December 1986): 825–42.

Jones, Mohamedu F. "President Taylor, His Wife (Wives), and the Marriage Laws of Liberia," *Perspective* (Atlanta, Ga.), October 24, 2002, http//www.theperspective.com.

Moore, Bai Tamia. "Problems of Vai Identity in Terms of My Own Experience," *Liberian Studies Journal* 15, no. 2 (1990): 10–12.

Moran, Mary H. "Woman and 'Civilization': The Intersection of Gender and Prestige in Southeastern Liberia," *Canadian Journal of African Studies* 22, no. 3, special issue: Current Research on African Women (1988): 491–501.

Nichols, Douglas, Emile T. Woods, Deborah S. Gates, and Joyce Sherman. "Sexual Behaviour, Contraceptive Practice, and Reproductive Health among Liberian Adolescents," *Studies in Family Planning* 18, no. 3 (May–June 1987): 169–76.

Ofri-Scheps, Dorith. "Bai T. Moore's Poetry and Liberian Identity: Offering to the Ancestors," *Liberian Studies Journal* 15, no. 2 (1990): 26–90.

Saunders, Janice M. "Liberian Higher Education at Cuttington University College: Are Both Sexes Equal?" *Liberian Studies Journal* 16, no. 2 (1991): 76–90.

Smyke, Raymond J. "Fatima Massaquoi Fahnbulleh (1912–1978): Pioneer Women Educator," *Liberian Studies Journal* 15, no. 1 (1990): 48–73.

———. "Nathaniel Varney Massaquoi (1905–1962): A Biographical Essay," *Liberian Studies Journal* 17, no. 1 (1992): 46–65.

7

Social Customs and Lifestyle

[I]n many of Liberia's indigenous cultures, the first draught of any alcoholic drink (in ancient times, palm wine) is spilled onto the ground, precisely as a consecrated offering to the ancestors.

—Dorith Ofri-Scheps, Liberian scholar[1]

Just as a government job is regarded as the best way to gain the protection of a patron, associating with a political party is seen as a conduit to patronage.

—John C. Yoder, Liberian political scientist[2]

GIVEN THE EVOLUTION OF the country from an amalgam of Americo-Liberian settlers and indigenous groups, and the resilience of traditional, Christian, and Islamic influences, social life and customs in Liberia are diverse and fascinating. Generally, indigenous and Western values coexist and intermingle. But by and large, there is an increasing trend toward the Westernization or Americanization of social life and customs. A blend of Western and African cuisine, dress, music, educational systems, and dance pervades the private and public spheres. Public educational institutions carry out instruction mainly in the English language, which has its local variants. The school curriculum includes lessons in local legends and folklore, and students have opportunities to promote their indigenous cultures through concerts and other cultural shows. In major cities like Monrovia, the capital, cinema houses serve as avenues for projecting popular culture.

This chapter highlights salient features of political culture, social life, and customs in Liberia from the past to contemporary times. Developments such as the protracted civil war and the demands of urbanization and modernity will be shown to have affected the traditional forms of socialization, leisure, and interactions. Urbanization has been a unifying factor, though it must be admitted that in Monrovia and other urban settlements, ethnic identification is still manifest. Hence, the various ethnic groups have their respective enclaves. Still, the common experiences of struggles for existence constitute a bond between ghetto dwellers and other Liberians in the urban centers. Liberian pidgin, sports, festivals, intermarriage, education, and leisure have cemented interpersonal relationships. The urban centers continue to be a hotbed of dissent as unemployed youth create their own subculture. There is thus a combination of frustration and fun in the desperate conditions of the urban centers.

CLASS AND STATUS

Although Liberia has been a republic since 1847, it began as and remains a country of cleavages. First, the Americo-Liberian settlers distinguished themselves from, and regarded themselves as superior to, the indigenous peoples that they met. All that changed with the coup of April 12, 1980. Second, even among the settlers, there was the distinction, based on the American southern plantation mentality, between the so-called house Negroes and the field Negroes. Accordingly, the former and their mixed-race masters settled in Monrovia and its environs, while the field Negroes were sent to settlements in

Woman of the Gola Tribe, near Zorzor, Liberia,
West Africa. © Topham / The Image Works.

Maryland and Sinoe counties. This explains why President Tubman faced initial opposition from the Americo-Liberian elite of Monrovia, because he was not from Monrovia or Mesurado County. Skin pigmentation was a second distinction among the settlers: the mixed-race settlers (mainly from Virginia and Maryland, who were reputed to be persons of means and education) were rated higher than blacks, and the first member of the latter group, E. J. Roye, who became president in 1871 was embroiled in a crisis that led to his assassination. But the party of his supporters, called the True Whig Party, became dominant for the rest of the period of Americo-Liberian ascendancy.

A third type of cleavage was that between the so-called civilized and the natives, roughly between those who were acculturated in the Western or American mold—usually literate and Christian, mainly Americo-Liberian—and those who were not. Because the settlers had already lost the essence of their African identity as slaves, they arrived with deep-seated prejudice against and contempt for the indigenous peoples of their new country. As the French did in their colonies through the policy of assimilation (which provided a means for willing and qualified colonial peoples to become French citizens), the Americo-Liberians incorporated selected civilized hinterland peoples into their establishment as clients. Many were assimilated into the families of leading Americo-Liberians and came to adopt new surnames (e.g., Barclay, King, Brisbane, Yancy) that reflected their new identities. Others got in through intermarriage, such as Henry Boima Fahnbulleh, whose marriage into a leading Americo-Liberian family ensured his rise to an ambassadorial post. Still others took to anglicizing their indigenous names: Wotor to Wotorson, Molly to Morris, Yekeh to Yekehson, Kollie to Kollyson, and Kpandeh to Kpandeson.

In the Liberian context, to be civilized is to imbibe or manifest a progressive or Western lifestyle, that is, an assortment of skills, values, and attitudes associated with a number of groups or agencies: the Americo-Liberians, the Christian missionaries, returnee migrants who had sojourned in any of the surrounding English and French colonies, and the intellectual elite of coastal West Africa. In Kpelle, to be civilized is to be *kwi*. In a sense, the division between the civilized and the native also reflects the difference between the white-collar worker and the peasant, and between the urban elite dependent on a regular income denominated in modern currency and the rural subsistence farmer still eking out a living from the land. Likewise, a number of occupations are readily associated with native (as opposed to civilized) women: subsistence farming and retail trading. However, it took much more than education to be considered civilized in Liberia from as early as the mid-twentieth century. The outward manifestation of one's inward conversion to the ideology of civilization included the quality and cost of one's dress, house, and home appliances. This clearly distinguished the civilized from the native or country, as known in Liberian popular expression.

A study of the capital city of Monrovia in the 1960s indicated that the class structure was organized around a civilized core.[3] The civilized section of the community was subdivided into three distinct groups arranged in a pyramidal order. At the apex were the elite and honorables, followed by the civilized in the middle, with the tribal or uncivilized at the base of the pyramid. The civilized comprised clerks, schoolteachers, nurses, and junior officials. Drivers, mechanics, domestics, technicians, and electricians occupied the transitional zone between civilized and tribal. Outside Monrovia, this unwritten class or social differentiation subsisted in the pre-1980 era and was reinforced even by the activities of formal groups known as civilized committees or civilized communities or elements, which existed to promote relations between the local elites and the central government. The Masonic societies and other esoteric groups, such as the Society of Oddfellows, Freemasons, United Brothers of Friendship, and Sisters of the Mysterious Ten, performed similar roles of acculturation.

The dress style, for instance, distinguished a native woman from her civilized counterpart: the former wore indigenous dress—referred to colloquially as tying lappa (wrapper)—while the latter was identified with Western dress. Indeed, the so-called lappa woman was a stereotype referring to the wrapper-tying native woman; the lappa wife was the country woman who was the other wife of the nonresident civilized husband. Such distinctions were formalized by a Christian denomination that classified the dues payable by its members supposedly to reflect the income of its members. Civilized women paid a higher rate than their native counterparts, a false dichotomy in the sense that some native women were richer than civilized ones and could well afford to buy the Western dress worn by the latter. It is instructive that civilized women who lost their white-collar jobs often survived by taking to retail trading, thus becoming native.

For the Kpelle, the *kwi-nuu,* or civilized person, was one who could manage or conduct civilized matters. He or she was characterized by his or her speech (English) and sartorial style—wristwatches, trousers, and shoes—as contrasted with that of the yokel. To be civilized in other respects and lacking command of the English language fell far short of the ideal and exposed one to ridicule for deficiency in so-called civilized manners. A civilized person was associated with Monrovia, the capital city, which was called a civilized town (*kwi-taa*). Since Monrovia epitomized civilization, knowledge of its ways even by the unlettered conferred a modicum of civilization. Against this changing concept of sophistication, possession by the *zoes* of traditional knowledge regarding the mysteries of the forest, for instance, was no longer esteemed but was considered superstitious and retrogressive in the modernizing Liberian society of the twentieth century.

Later, however, especially since the April 1980 coup, hinterland indigenes (who were ordinarily native or country persons) have asserted their native identity even after crossing the threshold to civilization through education, employment, assets, and exposure to foreign influences through travel. The civilized natives demonstrated their identification with their native roots by speaking their indigenous languages and participating in tribal cultural activities. Hence, they exemplified the reality of duality that had come to characterize the identity and personality of the indigenous African elite of Liberia. In other ways, the distinction between the two categories has been blurred, with each group crossing the supposed barriers that separated it from the other. Thus, the native can go to church like the civilized, while the civilized can consult a local diviner as does the native. That said, formal and informal education is employed to foster the process of civilization, such as the formal school system on the one hand and the practice of living in the households of the civilized on the other.

Language use is both an index and a tool of social interaction and class distinction. Given the cultural and linguistic diversity in the country, English is the lingua franca of Liberia. However, as in other parts of the English-speaking world, more than one type of English is spoken in Liberia. One type is the Standard Liberian English (SLE) that is employed in official communication and in the media. It differs slightly from the official or standard English in other West African countries—Sierra Leone, Ghana, and Nigeria—because of the influence of American English. Another brand of English spoken in the country is Merico or Americo-Liberian, Brokes, Kwasai, Waterside, or Water Street English. These names suggest the geographical location of its speakers (Waterside) or their ethnic identity (Merico). This is peculiar to the Americo-Liberians, for whom it is the language of first choice at home and in other informal settings. The distant ancestry of this brand of English has been traced to the Black English of the southern United States.

A third form of English in common use is Liberian Pidgin English (LPE), which is generally spoken by other Liberians apart from Americo-Liberians. Though ultimately derived from both SLE and Merico, it has its distinctive flavor and is akin to Pidgin English spoken in other parts of West Africa. It differs from SLE and Merico in that it lacks gender distinction. LPE is distinguished by other characteristics: disregard for verb tense, absence of a distinction between singular and plural forms, nonusage of the definite article, and a propensity for adding "oh" or "dem" at the end of sentences. Like Black American English, it also drops consonants or adds vowels at the end of words. Kru Pidgin English (KPE) is the fourth type of English spoken in

Liberia. Similar to the Krio spoken in Sierra Leone, its development and spread derived from the seafaring activities of the Kru, for which they are well renowned. Speakers of these varieties of English are not mutually exclusive; indeed, many Liberians practice code switching, by which they speak any of these languages in the appropriate contexts. It is considered improper to speak any of them in the wrong contexts.

SPORTS AND LEISURE

Soccer is the most popular sport in Liberia, in spite of the magnitude of American influence on the country. Intercounty as well as school sports competitions are organized to develop sports and foster sportsmanship. Organized soccer has been played in Liberia since the early twentieth century. In the celebrated match of August 1927, a Liberian team, the Young Lions, reportedly beat a European team, then an unprecedented feat. The national soccer team, called the Probables, was constituted only in 1954; they were the forerunners of the current national team, the Lone Star. The current name was adopted in 1964, deriving from the single star in the Liberian flag that symbolizes the country's status as the only Black African Republic for a long time. The Lone Star achieved a major feat by leading the dreaded Black Stars of Ghana by three goals to one at halftime in a game played in Monrovia on January 8, 1964. Though the Liberians eventually lost the game 5-4, and also suffered a lone goal defeat in the return leg in Accra, they had won consideration as a respectable team.

In recent years, Liberia has emerged as a major force in African soccer in spite of the devastating seven-year war and the political instability of the post-1980 coup era. Much of the credit for this goes to George Oppong Weah, voted World Footballer of the Year in 1995, European Footballer of the Year in 1995, and African Footballer of the Year in 1989 and 1995. He was subsequently voted African Player of the Century. After playing for local Liberian and African teams such as Barolle, Invincible Eleven, and Tonnerre, he was engaged by leading European clubs—Monaco, Paris Saint Germain, and Olympic Marseille of France; AC Milan of Italy; Chelsea and Manchester City of the United Kingdom—between 1988 and 2001. During his active playing days, Weah inspired his Liberian compatriots, at a time that the country's future was in question, to fly the Liberian flag. He supplied uniforms to the national team and funded its activities, with the result that war-torn Liberia almost upstaged Nigeria, a leading soccer-playing nation, on the road to the 2002 World Cup competition in Japan and South Korea. Weah has accordingly won recognition as the country's goodwill ambassador and continues to be a role model for the youth of the country and the African continent.

It is significant that Weah and Mohammed Kallon, who constituted the core of the giant-killing Liberian team (it was the first team in Liberian history to defeat the Nigerian Super Eagles in a competitive match), played in the Italian Serie A, arguably the world's toughest soccer league. Their rare achievement has inspired Liberian and other African youth and also explains why soccer is the leading game in Liberia, unlike in the United States, where basketball and baseball are far more popular. Liberia is intimately tied with soccer in the course of its emergence as a modern nation-state. It is significant that Weah's exploits on the soccer pitch have earned him wealth, respect, and confidence such that he was the frontrunner in the presidential elections of October 2005 but lost the run-off election of November 2005, receiving 40 percent of the vote.

Although President Samuel Doe (1980–90) was largely responsible for the crisis that engulfed Liberia, he too deserves some credit for popularizing sports, especially soccer, in Liberia. He was such an enthusiast that he continued to play the game as president. It is reasonable to suggest that he contributed to the unprecedented interest of the Liberian press in sports, for his tenure witnessed the emergence of as many as eight newspapers that were devoted exclusively to sports coverage. President Doe's passion for football was demonstrated beyond any doubt in 1989, when he gave the national soccer team, the Lone Star, a staggering sum of $1 million for achieving the unprecedented feat of defeating their Ghanaian counterparts, the Black Stars, admittedly a leading team on the continent, in a nontournament game.

Cinema, television, and festivals constitute avenues for relaxation for Liberians. Though there is some local content, most cinema and television programs reflect the impact of Westernization on the country. Moviegoers are generally young, whereas television is a source of education, information, and relaxation for the family. Religious ceremonies and public holidays provide occasions for festivities. The most notable public holiday (Independence Day) is July 26, which commemorates the country's independence in 1847. Religious festivals, such as Christian Easter and Christmas, and Muslim festivals, especially Eid-el-Fitr (which follows the Ramadan fast), are marked with great festivities—music, dancing, and feasting.

TRADITIONAL AND MODERN SOCIALIZATION

The process of socialization in Liberian communities varies from one community to another. Among the Kpelle, for example, the pattern was to indulge children until they attained the age of 2 years, after which they were trained by threat or ridicule. After the 6th year, children were subjected to occasional corporal punishment. Between the ages of 7 and 20, they were made to pass

Street child selling chewing gum in front of a wall decoration of Santa Claus, who is holding a cell phone and saying "Season's Greetings" (September 2, 2001). © Mikkel Ostergaard/VISUM/ The Image Works.

through the Poro or Sande bush schools, which used to last for upward of 4 years in ancient times, but the duration is now much shorter. The initiation that took place during the seclusion in the Poro and Sande schools involved clitoridectomy and labiadectomy for girls.

In premodern times, initiation into Poro and Sande as a vital aspect of socialization was compulsory for members of Liberian communities. Pressure was exerted to ensure conformity, often by open ridicule. A male noninitiate was called a small boy regardless of his age, or abused as a stupid person. Among the Loma, such a person was seen as merely an image or a shadow, having no substance. On the other hand, no man would think of marrying a woman who had not been initiated into Sande. A male noninitiate was subject to indignity at every turn, being made to run undignifying errands, such as carrying loads for his peers and chasing birds from the rice fields. Expectedly, he could not marry, own property, or hold public office.

Young boys and girls were required to go through the process of initiation, during which they attended the so-called bush schools. The schools were the principal instrument for integrating adolescents into the community of adults. The teaching entailed separate sessions in farming, basketry, weaving, fishing, cooking, the mysteries of herbal medicine, hunting, rules of etiquette, homemaking, and sex education. The period of confinement also inculcated the virtues of discipline, obedience, endurance, patience, and ability to work with others. The Poro *Dazo* was the chief executive or headmaster of this educational institution. Whenever the bush school was in session, the Poro proclaimed a ban on wars in all the ethnic groups in the Poro areas. Poro served other social purposes in war and in peace. It employed symbols and signs to transmit messages or to give warnings. Its sign language enabled members across a wide geographical area to communicate their membership and rank, which entitled them to certain privileges. Certain objects were also employed to authenticate the identity of envoys or to seal a pact. White kola nuts were presented to indicate peace and pure intentions during the negotiation of a treaty or an alliance.

In contemporary times, the Poro and Sande have lost their traditional grip on the socialization process. It is no longer possible to enforce initiation, and the impact of Islam, Christianity, and Western education has eroded their influence further. The Mandingo, in particular, resisted incorporation into the Poro/Sande cultural complex of their Kpelle hosts. In any case, the hostility was mutual in that the Kpelle *zo* saw the Muslim clerics and diviners as undermining their spiritual monopoly with their supposedly more potent charms and medicine. Orthodox Muslims based their opposition to initiation into Poro and Sande on the Quranic strictures against the violation of the central Islamic doctrine of monotheism (*shirk*), as opposed to the polytheism of indigenous religion. However, the practice persists in the rural communities, where conservative values have proven resilient. With the demand of secular, formal education, it is no longer feasible to keep initiates for three to four years. Hence, the time spent in the seclusion of the bush schools has been shortened to two or three weeks, making the exercise more symbolic and perfunctory than was the case in earlier times.

The monopoly of Poro and Sande in the education of youth in most parts of Liberia was broken by the schools established by the Muslim and Christian missions and the Liberian national government. Mandingo Muslims, for example, established Quranic schools along the trade routes where they settled. They attracted patronage because the schools taught their pupils Arabic and the Quran, and also because the non-Muslim peoples of the Liberian hinterland tended to attribute the commercial success of the Mandingo to their Islamic education and religion. This made Islamic schools competitive even against the Western schools, which were, for a long time, too few to make a significant impact. The result was that well into the late twentieth century, the socialization process in Liberia was the joint responsibility of indigenous, Christian, and Islamic educational institutions.

Formal, secular education, television, the Internet, and the cinema are modern agents of socialization, especially in the urban setting. To be sure, these facilities are concentrated in the urban centers, and their functionality is further restricted by the limited supply of electric power. Hence, access to the Internet and television is limited, as in other parts of West Africa. Students of tertiary institutions are the avant-garde of the modern culture borne on the wings of globalization. In dress style, music, diet, and aspirations, Liberian youth have become highly Westernized, like their counterparts in other parts of the global south. They prefer Western family structures (monogamy and the nuclear family), and many are widely traveled. A large Liberian émigré community exists in the United States, especially as a consequence of the civil war, and its members exert direct and indirect political, social, and economic influence on their homeland.

OCCUPATION, PRESTIGE, AND STATUS

As in other West African countries, Western education is highly regarded in Liberia for the access it gives to public-sector jobs and political appointments. The relatively low literacy rates mean that the relatively few Western-educated elite are privileged in a society where they have a monopoly on the means of public enlightenment and policy formulation. Teaching as a profession still enjoys some prestige, particularly at the tertiary level, where university lecturers produce high-level human resources and are in line for the highest public offices in the land. They also mold opinion through the newspapers and their commentary on radio and television. Yet professional qualifications, especially in law and medicine, are highly coveted and respected. Such is the prestige accorded the medical profession that ordinary people assume that one has a degree in medicine upon being introduced as a "doctor". This suggests that a young medical practitioner is adjudged to have greater utility than another who has a Ph.D. degree in the humanities or natural sciences. Naturally, many parents want their children to acquire the title and practice medicine. As an extension of this popular perception of the medical profession, patients place great premium on injections as opposed to prescription drugs that are administered orally. Hence, rural folks in particular complain if they are not given an injection by a physician for even the commonest of ailments.

Whatever the students' areas of specialization, the educational system inculcates status consciousness in the graduates of tertiary institutions. They are given the impression of being prepared to ultimately take over from the current set of privileged people. Hence, the system implicitly leads students to focus less on skills acquisition than on expectations of enhanced status. This is to be expected where instructors in agriculture appear before their students in inappropriate apparel, such as formal suits, the symbol of privi-lege rather than of hands-on skills acquisition. It also shows that white-collar jobs, especially in the bureaucracy, are highly valued in Liberia.

SOCIAL LIFE AND ETIQUETTE

Traditional etiquette is preserved in the cultures of various Liberian peo-ples. Among the Belle of Lofa County, for example, it was customary to acknowledge a friend's assistance or act of kindness by formally visiting him or her early in the morning (at 5:30 A.M.) on the day after the act was done. It was considered an act of ingratitude if this was not done.

The Belle also developed traditional forms of communicating messages. Drum signals were used to warn of danger and other potential calamities. A horn was blown to alert the community to the outbreak of war, and an elephant tusk was sounded to herald the arrival of royalty.

Liberians are very gregarious and enjoy social gatherings such as parties. They have a peculiar handshake that entails snapping the middle finger of a friend's right hand with one's own thumb and third finger. This peculiar snap handshake is attributed to Americo-Liberian influence, and its origin has been traced to the days of the slave trade when slave owners often broke their slaves' fingers as a sign of their subjugation. On getting to Liberia, the Americo-Liberians adopted it to celebrate their freedom.

A related aspect of social life in Liberia is the wider definition given to the concept of brotherhood and sisterhood beyond that of biological relation-ship. In the religious context, members of Masonic lodges, Christian churches, and the Muslim community (*Ummah*) commonly refer to one another as brothers and sisters. This contrived relationship involves mutual help and unfettered access to one another's homes on social visits or for assistance. Muslims, for example, often break their fast at the homes of their brothers—with whom they share only religious affiliation—if they happen to be visiting in the evening when the fast is usually broken. This bond cuts across cleavages of class, ethnicity, nationality, residence, and income. Among Christians, the concept of godparents and godchildren also creates a nonbiological bond that helps to mentor younger people in the religious community and the wider society. Such a relationship is formed at the birth and christening of a child, when responsible elders are chosen to be the child's godparents. Usually, the godfather or godmother is a person of some social status whose political, social, or economic leverage in society will aid the subsequent development of the child. In certain cases, the godchildren might spend their formative years with their godparents. As in the case of strategic marriages, such relationships linked less-privileged families with powerful patrons, and rural landless families with urban-based landowning ones. In both cases, the artificial relationships provide emotional, political, or economic security.

An extension of this concept is the tendency for Liberians to get involved in the lives of their neighbors, friends, and close kin. It is the norm to ask after the welfare of a neighbor or friend during a casual encounter on the road. In that case, it is also expected that one will freely divulge one's personal problems and implicitly solicit advice on solutions to practical issues, such as a nagging ailment. The afflicted person is thus availed of free counsel on the most efficacious treatment or the latest information on a particular subject. However, there can be reticence if strangers are within earshot of the conversation or if it is perceived that the other person is responsible for one's predicament. What is also implied in the pattern of social relations is the tendency for people to engage in self-diagnosis with or without the aid of friends and relatives. People tend to share experiences of the potency of particular herbs, medications, or physicians. Usually, the indigenous medical practitioner is patronized before recourse may be had to the *kwii,* or orthodox medicine.

The protracted civil war of the 1980s and 1990s has dislocated long-established patterns of social relationships, with youths being more assertive vis-à-vis their elders. The war provided an excuse for those who wished to flee the humdrum existence on farms. Youths were beginning to question the wisdom of the elders, who seemed to be acting primarily in their own interests. As they fought in the various militias and had the monopoly of violence, the wartime acts of many youth soldiers constituted a desecration of long-standing values. They disrespected elders, desecrated shrines, and humiliated masked figures. As many as 20 percent of the combatants were children under the age of 17. They had joined one militia or another for a variety of reasons: in reaction to the persecution of their ethnic groups or family by the Doe government, to protect their families and themselves, out of sheer intimidation or conscription, because of the lure of money or material possessions, and in response to the urge to flee rural poverty. Besides the dislocations caused by the war, economic factors are also creating intergenerational tensions. With independent income from sugarcane from which a type of cheap gin is extracted, youth in Lofa County are said to have become disrespectful to elders.

With the war over by 1997, Liberia was no longer the same. Many child soldiers faced the challenges of reintegration into normal life as noncombatants. Full of regrets for the wartime atrocities that they had perpetrated under the influence of arrogance of power conferred by the possession of arms, vengeance, alcohol, drugs, fear, peer pressure, and the peculiar circumstances of the war, many of them went back to school, while others opted for a trade or farming. Although critics might dismiss such claims, many of them also found solace in their faith in God. Wartime actors with fearsome reputations, such as Prince Yormie Johnson and a man whose nom de guerre was General Naked Butt (so-called because he led a contingent of fighters who fought stark naked as an antidote to bullets), have found redemption in the Christian faith even to the point of being ordained as clergy. The depth and impact of such experiences can be judged only by the passage of time, but they appear to have had a healing effect on a traumatized populace.

GAMES AND FOLKTALES

Indigenous games aided the process of socialization of boys and girls, for whom different or common games were invented. Such socialization prepared children for the next stage in life: initiation into Poro or Sande and marriage. Games among children bridged the gap between private and public domains by enabling children to integrate into the larger community. They also helped the children come to terms with the challenges of life outside the home, the reality of peer pressure, and life as a game of survival in an ordered society. Folktales, songs, and games shaped the outlook of children and youths in the community. Common activities such as games also ensured the conformity of children and youth to the norms of the community or ethnic groups by reinforcing community values. Involvement in games built the character and confidence of children and enabled them to adjust to changing circumstances. They further helped children to articulate ideas; master the art of counting; and appreciate indigenous music, traditions, values, and customs.

Many games were developed to promote recreation and socialization in the various indigenous communities. The game of "Leopard's Rocks" among the Gola taught the skills of counting. It was based on the folklore of the counting test devised by the leopard to entrap and kill those who failed it. Where everyone else failed the test, the royal antelope (*gbalia*) passed it by counting lyrically and systematically. Another Gola game, of pests and the rice farm, played by boys and girls, involved attempts by most of the participants (children in the role of birds) to steal from the rice farm. However, any bird that got hit in the course of the foray was transformed to rice. The Vai game of "Mother, Give Me a Canoe" engaged a group of boys, one of whom attempts to break out of a circle formed by the linked hands of his compatriots, an exercise that tasks the energy of the participants.

Folktales were an additional means of socialization among the peoples of Liberia. They were told to reinforce teachings or warn of the dire consequences of certain acts. A popular folktale is that of the fox and the rooster. The fox was always afraid of the bird because of its comb and always ran away because, as he admitted to the rooster, he thought that the bird was carrying fire on his head. The rooster consequently assured the fox that the comb was harmless and encouraged the fox to touch it. However, on getting to know that the object of his fear had no bone, much less fire, in it, the fox mobilized his ilk to prey on roosters, a practice that persists to this day. On one level the tale rationalizes the relationship between the hunter and its prey in the animal kingdom, but it also warns against disclosure of sensitive information or the divulging of secrets that might prove fatal to the unwary. Another folktale with a didactic bent is about a king who decrees that everyone should kill their parents so that he can have absolute power over his subjects. But one person defies him by hiding his own parents. The tyrannical king then makes an impossible demand: that his subjects make a mat of rice grains for him to sleep on, and to transfer his farm from a distance to the outskirts of the town. While others are perplexed, the one who has hidden his parents goes to them for advice and is told what to do. Based on the old people's counsel, the king is told to supply an old rice mat as a sample for the new one he has requested; he is also told to dry up the river on the way to the farm so that his people can shift his farm to the desired location. The king can do neither of these, and his subjects are therefore rid of his impossible demands. The folktale is meant to teach the moral that the counsel of old people or elders is indispensable for the prosperity of a community.

DEATH AND FUNERAL RITES

Death and funeral rites occupy an important place in the life cycles of all Liberian communities. Among the Belle, the burial sites of the king, commoners, and blacksmiths were located at different places in the community. The king was buried in the town but his subjects were interred outside the community. Blacksmiths were buried beside their workshop or foundry. The *dazo* of the Poro was buried according to the rites of that sodality known only to its high-ranking officials. The same applied to the *mazo* of the Sande, whose interment was handled by the leading members of the group. Both the Belle and the Grebo took steps to ascertain the cause of death of a person before the burial of the corpse. If an established traditional test confirmed that the deceased had been a victim of witchcraft, or had engaged in an evil practice leading to his or her death, certain rites were performed to neutralize the evil and avert its negative effect on the community. However, if such persons passed the test, their corpses were buried in the common cemetery of the pure dead.

Islam and Christianity have influenced funerary practices in many parts of Liberia. Christians organize a wake on the eve of the interment, which takes place after a church service. The corpse is placed in a coffin, and prayers are offered at graveside before the interment takes place. Depending on the age of the deceased and the circumstances of their death and family, the preacher will give suitable admonitions relating to the hope offered to the dead in Christ while offering comfort to the bereaved. Eulogies are also common, especially if the deceased had made a mark in his or her lifetime. The funeral is accompanied by music and merriment after the burial service. For the Muslims, a wake is held at which Quranic verses are recited all night. The body is simply wrapped in a white shroud and buried after a graveside service conducted by the imam with the mandatory recitation of Quranic verses. After the interment, food is served as a sacrifice in honor of the dead.

In the aftermath of the death and burial of a member of the Kpelle community, for example, a 40th-day commemoration feast is organized. This can be expensive in that it involves lavish entertainment, including the engagement of singers and dancers. It is expected that this feast requires the sacrifice of a cow, the cost of which is unaffordable to poorer members of the community. The cost of the exercise means that not many can afford to hold the feast on the 40th day. On their part, Kpelle Muslims mark the 40th post-humous day with a public meeting at which Quranic recitation takes place, at the end of which a feast is held without the loud merriment of other religious groups.

The impact of Islam on the funerary practices of Liberian communities is perhaps best exemplified by the Vai, the most Islamized of all indigenous Liberian communities. Traditionally, burial could be delayed for several weeks; often, the corpse was buried and later exhumed for reburial. But by the 1970s, the Vai had adopted the standard Islamic practice of burial immediately after death. Moreover, the practice of ascertaining before burial whether the deceased was a witch was discontinued. Furthermore, funeral feasts were made to conform to the Islamic calendar: on the 3rd, 7th, and 40th days after death. Funeral food that used to consist of rice and red palm oil—which was considered to be the preference of the ancestors—has been changed to rice flour mixed with sugar. The meal is now merely symbolic, the gathering being held in acknowledgment of the death of a member of the community. The 40th-day feast also follows the pattern among the Kpelle as described earlier, in which the traditional festivity, singing and dancing that extended all night, now assumes a somber atmosphere with Quranic recitations.

TABOOS AND TOTEMS

As in other African societies, indigenous Liberians observed taboos and totems as part of their sociocultural belief system. The Belle, for example, never ate the very short banana, which was their fertility totem. Their totem animal was the leopard, and physical contact with its hide by a Belle was believed to be capable of making the person insane. Belle twins were forbidden to eat black deer. The Belle also believe that certain occurrences, like the sighting of a chameleon (*gebue*), the singing of the *gunbenyanda* bird, and the cry of an animal known as *kpoolo* in daytime, were omens of death. They also interpret the actions of a bird called *kolakpokpo* as bringing either good fortune or bad luck. If it walked past a man on the road, it portended evil, but if it ran ahead of a traveler, the act was considered a good omen for that person. The entry of a firefly (*kamukahn*) into a household and its sighting by the residents was considered an indication of the coming of an agreeable visitor or access to fresh meat the next day.

Certain taboos are observed in social relations. A common one is that one does not greet people or hand things to them with the left hand. The idea behind this is that the left hand, which is used to clean up one's body after defecation, is disreputable and cannot be used to communicate with persons of one's status or higher; such an act is taken as a sign of contempt or disrespect. It is also considered disrespectful to sneeze or cough without covering one's mouth in the public. Likewise, it is socially unacceptable to sell food without covering it, because flies would otherwise spread diseases by contaminating such foodstuffs. Hence, one must cover food or boil whatever food has to be eaten. Limes are included in the preparation of food to neutralize the effects of such disease-bearing germs.

POLITICAL CULTURE

Liberian political culture is a product of its history and reflects the characterization of the country as a high-context society. More emphasis is placed on the survival of the group and its leadership than on the sensibilities of the individual. Given the centrality of the leader to the survival of the system, criticism of the leadership is discouraged as having the potential to destroy the entire system. Any attempt to remove the leadership is taken as a fatal challenge to the system built around the leader. Accordingly, opposing views are treated as dissent that has to be suppressed for the good of the whole. The individual thus suffers for the sake of the stability of the group.

The Liberian political culture is founded on a patronage system, where there is a pecking order in which leaders disburse largess to retain the loyalty and support of lower-ranking members. The big man politician or bureaucrat cultivates the image of a rich, generous, and accessible leader who assists his clients in securing jobs, getting children into choice schools, reaching a higher government official for favors, and solving personal financial problems. As part of this image, the big man is an honored guest at marriage, funeral, and fund-raising ceremonies at which he displays his generosity. Such dispensation of patronage attracts media coverage, which boosts the political capital of the patron, especially if he is a highly placed person.

Given the practice of patronage, the Liberian political culture does not encourage accountability in public affairs. Generosity is esteemed at the expense of fiscal integrity. Nepotism is rife. Because clients expect their patrons to be rich, the public does not ask—or permit—questions about the source of the farms, motor vehicles, and big houses owned by the big man. Honest and diligent officials who do not dole out patronage are despised even by their relatives for their supposed stinginess and self-righteousness. Even in schools, churches, and other public or private organizations, people in positions to do so help themselves to the treasury without fear of public opprobrium. The result is that state resources are siphoned out through inflated contracts (with a built-in 10 percent kickback), padded wage bills, and fake invoices and redistributed in a wasteful manner through the patronage system. Corruption thus fuels underdevelopment and sustains a parasitic elite. Government is run as a racket where regulations are manipulated to extort money out of the citizens, justice is subverted in favor of favorites, and documents are forged to legitimize dubious transactions.

Another element of Liberian political culture, which complements the patronage system, is that of respect for hierarchy, which implies docility or submission to higher authority. This attitude of deference or submissiveness to superiors or the powerful in society is ingrained in the individual through the various means of socialization—the family, school (indigenous, Islamic, and formal), and the church. Wives, for example, are taught by their families to submit to and bear with their unfaithful husbands. Yet this system of obedience is underpinned by subtle threats of consequences of dissent, rewards, and sanctions. In the political sphere, control is maintained and dissent contained by blackmail or largesse, and in extreme cases by imprisonment and violence, including assault and murder. The culture of acquiescence thus fostered results in self-censorship and sycophancy in the media coverage of the deeds and utterances of the powerful. The supposed good works of leaders are praised to the high heavens while their malfeasance is unreported. As we have seen in chapter 3, the cost of displeasing the powerful is often too high to be risked by a journalist who has a large number of dependents. Yet when the political culture does not encourage criticism and when tolerance is promoted as a healing balm for the traumatized Liberian society, the consequence is that mistakes are repeated while fraud and incompetence reign unchallenged. Even so, this tolerance is often denied those outside the circle of a patron or members of his own ethnic group.

Notes

1. Dorith Ofri-Scheps, "Bai T. Moore's Poetry and Liberian Identity: Offering to the Ancestors," *Liberian Studies Journal* 15, no. 2 (1990): 73.
2. John C. Yoder, "Liberian Political Culture: The State, Civil Society, and Political Culture" (mimeo).
3. Merran Fraenkel, *Tribe and Class in Monrovia* (London: Oxford University Press, 1964).

References

Brown, David. "On the Category 'Civilised' in Liberia and Elsewhere," *Journal of Modern African Studies* 20, no. 2 (1982): 278–303.

Bundy, Richard C. "Folk-Tales from Liberia (In Abstract)," *Journal of American Folklore* 32, no. 125 (July–September 1919): 406–27.

Conteh, Al-Hassan. "Reflections on Some Concepts of Religion and Medicine in Liberian Society," *Liberian Studies Journal* 15, no. 2 (1990): 145–57.

David, Soniia. "'You Become One in Marriage': Domestic Budgeting among the Kpelle of Liberia," *Canadian Journal of African Studies* 30, no. 2 (1996): 157–82.

Fraenkel, Merran. *Tribe and Class in Monrovia.* London: Oxford University Press, 1964.

Handwerker, W. Penn. "Technology and Household Configuration in Urban Africa: The Bassa of Monrovia," *American Sociological Review* 38, no. 2 (April 1973): 182–97.

Holsoe, Svend E. "The Dynamics of Liberian Vai Culture and Islam," *Liberian Studies Journal* 12, no. 2 (1987): 135–48.

Johnson, S. Jangaba M. "The Traditions, History, and Folklore of the Belle Tribe," *Liberian Studies Journal* 1, no. 2 (1969): 45–73.

Moore, Bai T. "Categories of Traditional Liberian Songs," *Liberian Studies Journal* 2, no. 2 (1970): 117–37.

Moran, Mary H. "Woman and 'Civilization'": The Intersection of Gender and Prestige in Southeastern Liberia," *Canadian Journal of African Studies* 22, no. 3, special issue: Current Research on African Women (1988): 491–501.

Nichols, Douglas, Emile T. Woods, Deborah S. Gates, and Joyce C. Sherman. "Sexual Behaviour, Contraceptive Practice, and Reproductive Health among Liberian Adolescents," *Studies in Family Planning* 18, no. 3 (May–June 1987): 169–76.

Ofri-Scheps, Dorith. "Bai T. Moore's Poetry and Liberian Identity: Offering to the Ancestors," *Liberian Studies Journal* 15, no. 2 (1990): 26–90.

Yoder, John C. "Liberian Political Culture: The State, Civil Society, and Political Culture" (mimeo).

8

Music and Dance

Music, an integral part of [Liberian] societies, . . . responded to changes in the socio-religious climate, substantiating the [assertion that] . . . "music follows culture."
—Lester P. Monts, musicologist and anthropologist[1]

As IN other aspects of Liberian culture, music and dance also manifest the duality of source and inspiration (indigenous and foreign), as well as the diversity of indigenous traditions and practices. In this chapter, the two related themes of music and dance are examined under two broad headings relating to provenance: the indigenous and the modern, with due attention paid to their constituent elements. However, attention is paid to the impact of Christianity and Islam, foreign elements that have been indigenized by Liberian peoples. The discussion also highlights the contributions of Liberia's cultural ambassadors in music and dance.

Traditional or indigenous Liberian music is akin to that of other West African countries in the combination and utilization of vocal repetition, poly-rhythms, ululation, and call-and-response. It is performed with dance and instrumental accompaniment on special occasions (birth, marriage, royal installation, festival, and funeral) and in everyday activities (work and play). Islam has made inroads into Vai and other indigenous cultures and has thereby affected secular and religious music in those communities. Christian music came with the missionaries and has been spread by the Americo-Liberian Christian community. However, many Christian songs are now composed in indigenous languages, and church music combines West African rhythms, the indigenous call-and-response format, and American harmonies. Modern music has been influenced by highlife, a popular musical genre dominant in West Africa since the 1950s that combined Latin American dance rhythms, African and Western instruments, and indigenous melodies and lyrics. It spread across coastal West Africa between Ghana and Sierra Leone, with a Liberian people, the Kru, being a major intermediary in its popularization.

INDIGENOUS MUSIC AND DANCE IN LIBERIA

Varieties of Indigenous Music

For clarification, the discussion in this section will focus on indigenous Liberian songs and dance associated with the indigenous peoples of the hinterland. To be sure, the Americo-Liberians brought a different brand of music and dance, deriving from their background in the Americas. Such music consisted of church hymns, patriotic songs, and popular dance music, which, being heavily Western oriented, will not be discussed here.

Each ethnic group in Liberia has its own repertoire of indigenous music, including songs for different occasions that serve various functions.[2] The lyrics of the songs contain historical data on developments in the family and the wider society. The songs capture significant moments or events in the personal lives of the composers or performers, or of their communities; they celebrate life or lament death; they are associated with pleasure and work, with politics and ritual. In short, indigenous songs relate to the phases in the life cycle of the individual and the vicissitudes of larger entities such as the family and ethnic group. Birth, death, sports, secular and religious education, and the transmission of folktales have special songs associated with them.

Among the Gio (Dan), who straddle the Liberian/ Côte d'Ivoire border, music making is a respectable profession that runs in families. Traditionally, musicians were attached to chiefs, warriors, wrestlers, secret societies, and professional associations, and they plied their trade from place to place. Their instruments comprised gourd rattles, mortar and slit drums, and bells. The Gio combine drums and ivory trumpets to produce music, which often accompanies masked dancing. Their music may be classified into three groups: *zloo* (praise song), *tan* (dance song), and *gbo* (funeral dirges). *Tan* is the most prevalent type of music, but while its text is fairly fixed, that of *zloo* is open to improvisation, given the nature of its subject and audience.

The Kpelle too have professional musicians, who also double as subsistence farmers or laborers. These *ngulei-siyge-nuu* (the song-raising persons) perform at receptions, funerals, and festivals. Women perform as soloists while men function as storytellers, singers, and instrumentalists. Kpelle instruments are similar to those of the Gio; they consist of the xylophone (*bala*); the flute (*boo*); the sideblown horn (*turu*) made of ivory, wood, or animal horn; rattles; and various types of the slit drum. Kpelle music is played on various occasions: initiation into Poro and Sande, harvest, games, work, holidays, and masked dancing.

Liberian peoples developed different genres of music for different daily or seasonal activities. The songs originated from different ethnic groups, reflecting their occupational specialization, and diffused across ethnic frontiers. Thus, the Dei, Gola, Vai, and Mende have a large repertoire of songs for work, recreation, and entertainment. Rice songs are composed in Mende and Vai because those groups are associated with the early development of agriculture, whereas hunting songs are mainly rendered in Gola because hunting was the primary occupation of that group. However, each ethnic group has a collection of songs devoted to specific topics dealing with their respective lore and folktales.

The Kru of southeast Liberia are a famous seafaring people whose apparent homogeneity has been forged in the course of their maritime migrations and service on European and American ships. Their traditional music is predominantly vocal, with the accompaniment of a wooden drum (*tuku*) and other instruments of percussion. It consists of warrior songs and a collection of songs known as *si-o-lele,* songs rendered by women's associations at social gatherings and funerals in a chorus-refrain format. This genre of songs achieved popularity among other Liberian groups and even across West Africa from the mid-twentieth century.

Music and Dance in Daily Life

Music and dance depict various daily and seasonal activities from the cradle to the grave in indigenous Liberian societies. As in other human communities, the birth of a child—regardless of gender—was celebrated by the infant's parents as well as their kinfolk and acquaintances. Songs heralded the birth of a child as the mother was perceived to have fought a battle with death to bring the child to life. Joyous shouts (of *hoyoo, hoyoo*) usually greeted the delivery of the baby inside a *zo* house or an enclosure made by a fence. Such songs were often improvisations, but others were quite common and associated with particular ethnic groups. The Gola, Bandi, Grebo, Gio, and Vai have indigenous lullabies that are rendered to pacify babies or lull them to sleep. Lyrics of the various songs contain information about the mothers' activities and give the impression that the babies understand why they are not receiving due attention. A Bandi cradle song contains these lyrics:

Little child don't cry
Your mother is gone to fish

She will catch a big crab
For us to roast and eat.

This is similar to another in the Gio language:

It is wrong for a nursing mother to run about
It is wrong to pass your child from hand to hand.

Songs are also an accompaniment to children's games, an essential element of indigenous education and socialization. The games and the attendant songs reflect the challenges of daily life, such as protecting the rice crop from birds, or reinforcing some qualities of character, such as wisdom. The Vai game of "Mother, Give Me a Canoe" is accompanied by a song rendered by the boy trying to break out of a circle formed by the linked hands of his compatriots. The song that he sings during the game contains the following lyrics:

Mother, give me a canoe
There is no canoe
Mother, give me a paddle
There is no paddle
If I see a canoe and paddle anywhere can I take them?

As he sings, his compatriots respond with the refrain "yes" as he attempts to detach their linked hands. This game and song combination is paralleled by the Grebo "Kpako Ate the Money," which is played by both boys and girls, all singing "Kpako ate the money" repeatedly.

Liberian communities also composed and rendered work songs that accompanied farm tasks including the clearing of the farm site, tree felling, burning of residue, weeding, planting, and harvesting. Such tasks required cooperative effort that was made more efficient by musical accompaniment. The Kissi of Lofa County composed the following song rendered by a party of girls engaged in weeding:

How many of you are there?
We are ten, do not forget to call our names.

While the leader sang the first line, the others, who were engaged in weeding, chanted the other line as a refrain. Among the Gio, a member that engaged a cooperative work group, known variously as *demu* or *kuu,* also engaged a musician to entertain the workers. A common song for motivating such a work group while it cleared the farm site goes like this:

Hoo e wende I yoo
Hoo wee

Hoo e wende I yoo
Hoo wee

The first line of the song was sung by the leader of the group while the members sang the next line as a refrain. Although the lyrics are not capable of systematic translation, they are meaningful to the workers, who are reputed to have been sufficiently galvanized by the song to work nonstop for hours on end. Among the Kru of southeastern Liberia, songs were rendered to accompany the felling of trees and the planting of rice. For tree felling, the following song was rendered:

I am going to fell a big tree
If I do not fell a big tree, I will not have a wife.

It is significant that tree felling, an index of masculinity or an indication of farming prowess, was considered a prerequisite for matrimony. The motivational power of matrimony or chivalry in songs can be deduced from another Liberian work song attributed to a Kissi composer, Tamba Foloba of Kolahun:

I do not care how ugly a woman may be, just so her waist feels young
When a woman tells you "no," quite often she means yes
The Bandi girl calls me, "Sabai, come let us eat rice."
They fail to realize that I do not speak Bandi
Tamba Sengi ate so many eggs till he began to cook them with cassava
   leaves
A bald-headed man does not like to fight in the night for fear he might
   get hit on the head.

Matters of everyday life are captured in secular songs known variously as *Yombo, Dendia, Kolako* or *Baa, Waya,* and *Lemgbe* by the Gio, Dei, Bassa, Palipo, and Gola, respectively. Such songs conveyed counsel, ridicule, gossip, and praise and concerned mundane matters like love affairs, emotions, and marriage. Love was a dominant theme in many indigenous songs of this type, which commented on disappointments in love and counseled against infatuation. A Gola song of the 1920s recorded how girls seeking to court Fahn Wasa, a most eligible bachelor of the times, offered him what turned out to be the wrong dish. The faux pas was stated in the following lyrics:

We cooked butter beans for Wasa to eat
Wasa does not eat amulets.

The reference to amulets derived from the resemblance of small beans to the amulets made by Muslim diviners that were worn on the body for protection against spiritual attacks. The theme of disappointed love was also pursued in a Vai love song composed by one Bondokai Zoogboo:

> If you find a dry raffia branch in a canoe, row with it
> You met me with my running about and you said you loved me
> You met me very promiscuous and you said you loved me.

This was a clear warning against infatuation and its consequences. Jealous or possessive husbands were also lampooned in songs such as the following in the Palipo language of the Grand Gedeh County, entitled "Gbo ba bli":

> People who went to Fernando Po rowed back and enjoyed their freedom
> People in prison should be given their freedom
> Women must have their freedom to go out and play (dance)
> President Tubman has given us freedom, we got to play.

This song also contains historical and social information of great significance. The reference to Fernando Po relates to the forced labor scandal that made Liberia a pariah nation in the 1920s and 1930s, when peoples of the hinterland were sent to virtual slavery on the Spanish-held island of Fernando Po. Alluding to that episode, the song stated that while the people exported to Fernando Po and even convicts regained their freedom, wives of possessive husbands remained in bondage. The song can be dated to the period 1944–71, when President William V. S. Tubman was president of Liberia, and might be an endorsement of his policy toward the hinterland peoples. The song thus contains social commentary with a wider ramification than the mundane issue of matrimony. The jealous husband motif is also present in the following Gola song of unknown antiquity:

> I have closed my book
> If you do him so
> That jealous man has not gone to sleep
> When that thing goes to sleep I will slip out, Lover
> If you do him so
> That stupid fellow is the one the rains will beat
> I have closed my book
> When that thing goes to sleep I will slip out, Lover.

Generally, human foibles or follies are criticized in Liberian indigenous songs, drama, and dance. A Vai song of the 1920s ridiculed women who struggled to appear younger than their age. This was long before the age of bleaching creams and dyed hair. The lyrics of the song are very explicit:

Old woman with white hair
You are not a young mother
But you cannot take your hands from Fanti prints.

The song alluded to the penchant of fashionable middle-aged women for acquiring English cloth, known locally as Fanti cloth. It indicates societal disapproval of women who did not dress according to their true age or who appeared to be competing with the younger generation for the good things of life. The tendency for society to suppress the femininity of the aging female is further implied in the song. The image of the typical woman is also conveyed in songs such as the following Gola song, entitled "Jama":

A woman is like a vine, which creeps up on any tree
A woman is like a gun barrel, every man suits her
A woman is like a diamond creek, one has to test her to make sure
A woman without training talks about men.

The typical woman was thus pictured as dependent upon, and easily manipulated by, men and yet not really reliable. An ideal woman was not supposed to be preoccupied with men. Such views reflect the sexist chauvinism of a traditional patriarchal society.

Yet women's feelings are also captured in popular songs, such as "Ba Nya M Go Koma," the Gola *Lemgbe* (folk song) that became a popular hit tune of the mid-1950s. That song captured the defiance of childless women, whose plight does not elicit sympathy in a patriarchal society that is obsessed with procreation as the essence of marriage:

Ba nya m go koma o
E koma je jee
Ba nya m go koma o
M jei yei Gola
Mfe goye joa nyu ndo
By nya m go koa o
Ekoma je jee
Ba nya m go koma o
M jei yei

Its English version is as follows:

I will rear nobody's child
They said I had no child

To have a child is painful
They said I had no child
So I will sit down so.[3]

Common features of human character and observations of regular occurrences in society are recorded in indigenous songs of Liberian peoples. A song
by Luopu, a popular female Loma singer, succinctly captured in the following
lyrics some generalizations about human conduct:

A poor man cannot afford to get angry
A poor man has no friend behind him
Where you visit often is where your heart is
A man without family is not a man
If you have a grown daughter, plenty young men will come
To say hello to you
The day she goes away you have less company.

Another song in the Dei language recorded in 1965 also noted certain regu-
larities in human life, including the phenomenon of cause and effect, the
capacity of a chance spark to lead to a great conflagration, and the prospect of
a piecemeal approach to achieve great results:

Haul rope and rope will haul bush (trees)
If there is noise under a monkey he cannot rest
If something is under a matter, that matter cannot finish
What secret is there a *zo* cannot tell?
Taking a thing away one by one finishes it.

Songs are also composed to commemorate significant historical events or to
praise celebrated personalities such as the Liberian president and paramount
chiefs, or to salute great accomplishments. The invention of the Vai script in
1814 and its formal presentation to the sovereign of the Gawula kingdom
elicited the composition of a song in honor of the inventor, Dualu Bukele.
The song, which became the Vai anthem, was revised after Liberia's independence in 1847:

Expression of joy
I am a young leopard, take me to a king
Oh the small tree, the tree has become a big one
Liberia's lone star has shown us light
Hail, hail, our father's labors have not been in vain.

The military exploits of an undefeated nineteenth-century Gola chief, Kpomakpolo of Kle, whose stronghold was invincible, were eulogized by Gola women in the following song:

> Carry me to Kle
> Carry me to Kle
> If you are (a) man carry me to Kle
> Carry me to Kle
> The guns of Kle sound like cannons
> Carry me to Kle
> Carry me to Kle
> If you are (a) man carry me to Kle.

Indigenous music in Liberia covered religious as well as secular themes. The initiation of boys and girls into Poro and Sande, respectively, a significant rite of passage in indigenous culture, was accompanied by songs capturing or announcing the various stages of initiation. The following song, originally in Gio, heralded the commencement of the Poro initiation:

> We have gone into the bosom of a *doo* tree
> We have set our raffia leaf curtain in the entrance of the grove.

This signaled that women and noninitiates could not enter the grove to know the secrets of the conclave. Shortly before the conclusion of the Poro initiation, the *ziawa* dance of the Dei, Gola, Mende, and Vai was usually performed by men and women. Ziawa songs commented on the plight of the rice farms of parents whose children were undergoing initiation or the fate of a young woman who defied the Poro. Sande songs taught the girls personal discipline, such as waking up early, as indicated in a Kissi song:

> Head of the Sande girls the day is dawning
> Be brave, everything will be all right.

Other songs captured their feelings and thoughts as initiates, such as this Vai song:

> I am sitting here
> I don't have anyone
> I did not know it
> Zowo kpemgbe they have finished initiating you.

Death as a universal human experience is also featured in indigenous funeral songs. Every ethnic group has its own repertoire of funeral dirges. Poro men sing the following song at the funeral of a Kpelle *zo*:

> *Zemgbe tuule* let us go to the high forest
> You who doubt, Poro has put on full regalia.

Among the Palipo of Grand Gedeh County in southeastern Liberia, in a region without the Poro tradition, the following song, entitled *Aa dakpa o,* gives a vivid imagery of the transience of life and the inevitability of death:

> We come here as strangers
> The way we come here, we are strangers
> The person who came as a stranger has gone back
> We are all strangers, we will all go someday.

The painful loss occasioned by the death of a loved one is reflected in a Bassa funeral dirge:

> Banwon has died I will not see him again
> Gion has carried my mother and father away
> I will never see them again
> With whom will I stay?

Real-life personal experience of the loss of an only child was related in the moving dirge composed by Mole Punga, wife of a Lofa County paramount chief. Her personal grief and deep anguish are recorded in the following immortal lyrics:

> Every woman likes to have someone (a child) walk behind them
> How can I lie down and my side reach the mat pallet,
> When my only child is in deep slumber?
> You lying down, the pepperbird is crying and you cannot get up
> I am up most of the night, thinking of my child
> So is life, anything can happen in this world
> I do not know why God did this to me.

Indigenous music both secular and religious has generally been accompanied by dance. This was especially so in the case of the Poro and Sande. The arts of music and dance were taught as part of the initiation of youngsters into these secret societies. Usually, noninitiates were already familiar with the various songs rendered by themselves or by their elders in the course of daily activities. In one category were game or play songs rendered by children for recreation.

The other comprised those sung by older persons while fishing, hunting, or pounding foodstuff on the mortar. Children often rendered the songs without appreciating the proper contexts for them, but they soon acquired proper knowledge of their usage in the course of their initiation into the various societies. Hence, their outing ceremony upon their initiation was characterized by a public dance performance.

The initiates danced to music produced by the talking drum (*gihn*)—played by their trainer, referred to as *kembe* (uncle) for the Poro or Beli and *kengai* for the Sande—and other instruments, and lyrics rendered by the women. The initiation of girls into Sande involved intensive training in dancing and singing. Those who excelled in training performed on the occasion of the outing of the initiates. The Sande girl initiates danced to songs depicting daily activities such as cooking, farming, fishing, body adornment, and collection of wild honey. Sande members regarded dance as much more than a gymnastic or physical exercise. It was meant to offer entertainment and instruction, and its performance combined lucidity, beauty, and significance. Dancing involved the coordinated movement of the body and limbs to convey some philosophical truths often lost on the noninitiates.

It is significant that the Sande society also had its masked spirit-impersonator (*zoo-ba*), who played an important role in the society's ceremonies and rituals, a rare example of female masked dancing in Africa. Their Beli counterparts were constituted into a troupe, called *wusa,* which performed a spectacular acrobatic dance. Thus, in various indigenous Liberian communities, songs and dance featured in the performances of masked dancers who represented the public faces of the various secret societies. Masked dancers performed at public occasions in towns and villages to songs in the various indigenous languages.

The musical-dramatic folktale of the Kpelle, known as the *meni-pelee,* illustrates the blend of music, dance, and drama in Liberian society. Usually performed to large audiences on a market day, it involved a master storyteller and music by soloists and chorus singers. The audience too participated in the musical drama as everyone was familiar with the theme and lyrics. The story line is didactic, teaching certain morals and reinforcing societal values and communal traditions, such as family bonds and obedience to conventions and natural laws. Beyond its didactic function, the *meni-pelee* was also meant to entertain, for which purpose the storyteller was given the liberty to employ the devices of hyperbole, onomatopoeia (making sounds to convey meanings), dramatic facial and hand gestures, interjection of explanation, body movement, repetition, and suspense to enliven the atmosphere.

In general, indigenous music and dance tended to be localized in the ethnic or linguistic group in that each song or dance reflected the particular experiences of their composers. Moreover, religious songs and dance had to conform to an established standard and were therefore not susceptible to significant changes. In contrast, secular music and dance changed with the times even if they proved resilient in many cases. Yet, though all songs and dances were infused with the local idioms of the various language groups, some of them did cross the barriers of ethnicity and language. For example, *Sio le le,* a popular Kru song, was developed into a popular Vai anthem by the early 1960s.

Unlike in Muslim societies of Sudanic Africa, musicians and entertainers were not despised or accorded a low social ranking in Liberian communities. Rather, practitioners of the art were accorded recognition and respect above blacksmiths, weavers, and carvers. Yet, in communities with Poro/Sande institutions in the northern and central regions of Liberia, the blacksmith was often the *zo* of the prestigious institution of Poro.

Music and dance also enjoyed political or royal patronage in communities that had the chieftaincy institution. Such communities had court musicians who were clients of paramount and clan chiefs, and it was not unusual to find them in the retinue of a chief wearing leopard-skin costumes adorned with cowrie shells. Secular and religious music was accompanied by the use of instruments such as the talking drum and the indigenous hand piano (*kongoma*). The Belle invented the *tandegi* or *fanga,* a musical instrument deployed in wartime to challenge warriors to fight valiantly. Various drums and other instruments known as the *samgba, sasaa,* and *konigi* (which belonged originally to the Loma) were employed to produce music by the Belle and other Liberian peoples. New instruments were added as Liberian peoples encountered external influences. The widely traveled Kru mariners, for example, incorporated the acoustic guitar into the repertoire of their musical instruments. This was an improvement on their own plucked lute made of a calabash, a carved stick, and strings. Other instruments added to this ensemble were banjos, accordions, harmonicas, and concertinas. The Kru and the Grebo also introduced brass bands, which became popular along the Liberian coast in the late 1930s. The bands played a medley of African and European tunes.

ISLAMIC IMPACT ON MUSIC AND DANCE

Indigenous music in Liberia has been affected by external influences such as Islam, as in the case of the Vai, possibly the most heavily Islamized indigenous people of Liberia. Unlike in other parts of West Africa, the Islam that was introduced to the Vai neither introduced new musical instruments nor prohibited certain musical practices or the patronage of musicians by political leaders. The chanting that accompanied the Islamic call to prayers constituted a new musical element among the Vai. In addition, the early Muslim missionaries in the area introduced *suku* (from *shukran,* the Arabic for to give thanks), a musical genre in which the text was a combination of Arabic, Vai, and Koniaka languages. This brand of Islamic music did not borrow wholesale the Islamic musical style. Rather, it had West African features: complex rhythmic structures and a call-response mode of delivery. Still, it contained elements of Islamic music: Islamic songs and prayers, with typical Islamic chants and melodies, and changing postures and behavior during performance. Initially, the Islamic influence was limited to the call to prayers, Quranic chant, and ritual prayer. It did not extend to Vai songs that accompanied communal activities such as funerary processions or rice pounding.

But with the greater Islamization of Vai society in the late twentieth century, Islamic music displaced traditional songs in Vai funerary rites. Vai lyrics gave way to Islamic songs in Arabic or a combination of Arabic and indigenous languages. Where no indigenous songs had been rendered in the procession to the grave, Islamic songs were rendered praising Allah or Muhammad rather than eulogizing the dead or the ancestors. Generally, funeral dirges in Vai were displaced by chanted prayers and Quranic recitation.

Islam has also exerted profound influence on indigenous sacred music and dance of the Sande, especially among the Vai. Traditionally, musical instruction was an important element of the initiation of young men and women into the Poro (known as Beli among the Vai) and Sande, respectively. Group performances of dances and songs were taught to instill in the initiates a bond of unity. Among the Vai, for example, music in the indigenous brand of Sande (*zoo-ba* Sande) was accompanied by the use of *sasaa,* a gourd rattle, played by the women. Indeed, instruction in the mastery of the instrument was an aspect of training of Sande initiates. Among their male counterparts, talented ones were instructed in the use of a variety of musical instruments.

The Islamic influence on the indigenous sacred songs of the Poro and Sande took the form of a structural change in the performance of the music. The use of the gourd rattle (*sasaa*) supplemented the hand clapping that characterized the pre-Islamic mode of singing in the sacred lodges. However, the religious strictures characteristic of Islam also meant that performers were now less able to improvise in the use of lyrics, more so for Sande women who were not versed in Arabic. Either way, the songs were rendered in choral unison, involving a call-response format, with the leader rendering the more melodic line and the chorus being more often than not a repetition of the lead line. The Islamic impact has also entailed the prohibition of the masked spirit impersonator as well as the elaborate ritual for initiating a new *zoo-ba.*

Such has been the influence of Islam on the Vai that there has been a sharp decline in the number of traditional musicians among them, compared to other groups in which Poro and Sande exist, such as the Gola and Mende. Conversely, the increase in the number of Muslim rituals and celebrations has generated a distinct class of professional musicians known as the *sukuu-ba*. These have been trained in Quranic schools to perform at Muslim ceremonies.

Islamic music among the Vai is entirely vocal, with no Arabic-inspired instrumental accompaniment. This contrasts with the situation in the western Sudan, Ghana, and Nigeria. Emphasis is placed on vocal accomplishment. All the songs of *suku* must contain Arabic lyrics; otherwise they amount to worldly music (*don*). However, Quranic chants are not regarded as *suku*. Still, the composition of the Islamic songs is similar to that of non-Islamic Vai songs in that the composers enjoy a wide latitude of inventiveness and creativity. The lyrics comprise portions of the Quran or Islamic aphorisms, or expressions in Koniaka, Vai, and Arabic languages.

MODERN MUSIC AND DANCE

Modern music and dance exist side by side with their indigenous counterparts in Liberia. Often, as in the case of Kru music, the indigenous genre is modernized with most satisfactory results. The Kru achieved fame for their palm wine guitar style of music that also became popular across West Africa. This was an authentically African and innovative style based on a unique two-finger style of picking on the guitar, which was known in Nigeria as Krubass. Palm wine music, also called sea breeze music in Monrovia, was later developed by Americo-Liberians who replaced picking with strumming on the guitar. The Kru also exported their innovative music styles to Nigeria and Ghana. In the latter country, their *dagomba* acoustic guitar style exerted a great influence on its highlife music. Kru highlife music was a dominant influence in Nigeria in the 1940s and 1950s. It was based on experimentation with wind instruments, such as flutes and pennywhistles, and the organ and mandolin. Although the influence of Kru music declined steadily after the late 1950s, the palm wine guitar brand of music left an enduring impact on Nigerian and Ghanaian music. Two songs—"O gio te bo" ("She has come for it again") and "Si-o-lele"—were developed out of older Kru songs into great hits across West Africa and beyond. The tune of the former (shortened to "OGTB") featured in many popular songs of the 1940s and 1950s in Ghana and Sierra Leone.

Nontraditional music and dance have derived from Christian and Islamic traditions, as typified by the Americo-Liberians and the Vai, respectively. However, the Americo-Liberians came to Liberia with the church and Western traditions of music, while Islamic influence has percolated Vai traditional songs. Modern popular music, as distinct from the indigenous and religious types, had been prevalent since the middle of the twentieth century. During the Second World War (1939–45), an album was released by a popular Liberian folk musician, Baby Hayes. It contained the songs "Bush Cow Milk," "Nana Kru," "Jatu," and "Chicken is Nice with Palm Butter and Rice," among other numbers. The Greenwood Singers, a group of Liberian musicians, also released an album during the same period. In the 1950s, collections of indigenous songs drawn from the repertoire of various ethnic groups (Gio, Kpelle, Bassa, Loma, Kru, Vai, Gola, and Mandingo) were released as musical albums. Toni Saletan, a visiting American folksinger, collected and performed Liberian folk songs, including the evocative "All the Young Girls Running Down to the Airport" and others in indigenous languages. The song about young girls running to the airport captured the Second World War experience of young girls dating American servicemen stationed at Robertsfield airport.

The recording of Liberian indigenous songs during the 1960s was boosted by the availability of imported battery-operated tape recorders. The electronic gadget became a prized possession in the Liberian hinterland because it facilitated singing and dancing during feasts and festivals. Among the recording enthusiasts of that period was the Liberian cultural icon Bai T. Moore, whose recordings created a rich collection of indigenous music that soon filled the airwaves on the national radio station when it commenced broadcasting in indigenous languages in 1962. A special program, "Music of our Land," was soon introduced to air indigenous music. However, a religious broadcasting station, Radio ELWA, pioneered the broadcast of indigenous music by airing religious songs in the indigenous languages. It later included the broadcast of indigenous popular music of the genre indicated previously. The collection and preservation of indigenous music received official support when the government of Liberia funded a project to tour the indigenous communities of the Liberian hinterland to collect their folk songs. Members of the team included Leo Sarkistan and Bai T. Moore. An exhaustive two-year tour of the various regions and counties yielded a rich collection of songs that were compiled into a long-playing album entitled "Music Time in Liberia."

The decades since the 1960s witnessed the increasing influence of foreign music, notably Ghanaian highlife, American jazz, and Afro-Cuban music. None of these foreign brands succeeded in suppressing indigenous music and attendant dance forms, though the latter suffered some relegation. However, a new form of indigenous music emerged from an amalgam of the purely indigenous and the foreign. This was produced by talented musicians who became Liberia's cultural ambassadors.

LIBERIA'S MUSIC AMBASSADORS

From the 1970s, Liberia has produced a crop of outstanding musicians who developed into the country's cultural ambassadors. Notable names include Woyee, Jake D, Naser Sokay, Calvin Ward, Hawa Moore, Dehconte, and Miatta Fahnbulleh. Some of the hit tunes of this period include "A Yam Yam Sae," "Beautiful Family," and "Ya Monnue," each of which contains beautiful lyrics and conveys powerful messages.

Hawa Daisy Moore, a Vai-Liberian of royal pedigree, is a talented singer and songwriter. Raised by a Vai father and an Americo-Liberian stepmother, she was immersed in both the indigenous and Western/Christian cultures that shaped her career as a musician of international renown. Her initiation into Sande endowed her with the musical repertoire of her indigenous culture, but she also learned more from older relatives. A powerful influence was exerted by her father, whose knowledge of music and ability to play diverse instruments had been facilitated by his training by Christian missionaries. Hence, young Hawa received great impetus from an accomplished musician-father who himself played the guitar, grand piano, and tenor saxophone and was, in the 1950s, a member of the Greenwood Singers Band, which played a variety of indigenous and foreign brands of music at special government occasions. From an early age, Hawa exhibited a prodigious talent for composing and singing songs, which she taught to and sang with other children.

Hawa Moore was further exposed to the cultures of many indigenous Liberian peoples as she accompanied her father on his official tours. Residence in the capital, Monrovia, and in Cape Mount also acquainted her with Americo-Liberian church music and popular music from other African countries and the United States. Young Hawa soon began to record popular Liberian songs and her own compositions for radio and television. She led a 40-member band of schoolgirls, whose compositions and songs were aired on Christian and national radio and television stations in Liberia. Her appearance on television and at concerts gave her national prominence.

A turning point in her career was the encounter in 1977 with leading South African musician Miriam Makeba, who engaged her as a backup singer on her tour of Africa. Hawa Moore recorded her own songs on her return to Liberia, the last of which was released in 1989 on the eve of the country's descent into prolonged crisis. She fled to the United States in 1991 and has continued her career with the support of her husband and five children. In 1994, she founded the Akpandayah troupe to present West African music and dance to the American audience. She has been featured in various music and dance programs, including the Philly Dance Africa program of the Philadelphia Folklore Project. Hawa Moore has continued to project Liberian culture through live performances at various church and community events, concerts, and workshops on African music.

Joe Woyee, a drummer, songwriter, singer, producer, and arranger, an indigene of Greenville in Sinoe County, is another notable Liberian cultural ambassador. Raised by Western-educated parents, he learned to play the gui-tar as a child and cofounded the Fantastic Beginners, an elementary school band. When his parents moved to Monrovia, his musical career was further developed and he joined another schoolboy band called the Children of the Green Acres, in which he displayed his expertise in drumming. That band was distinguished by its composition of authentic Liberian popular music.

Moving to the United States in 1980, Woyee settled in Minneapolis and cofounded an international band, called Kairos, that played a unique brand of reggae. He later joined other musicians to establish the Out of Africa band. A multitalented artist, Woyee has composed songs for Kairos and Out of Africa, has produced music for the Voice of Liberia Band, and has written music for the Monga Band, a popular Liberian group. His major contribution has been the blending of various genres of music—blues, funk, smooth jazz, and Caribbean and African music—to create what he calls "rhythm and beat."

The talented pair of Jake Daynuah and Naser Sokay represent a unique breed of Liberian cultural ambassadors. Jake D, as the former is called, is a singer and percussionist whose brand of music combines diverse instruments and styles ranging from East to West Africa. Naser Sokay, a songwriter and singer who is married to Jake D, is associated with a genre of music called Sokay, from the title of her 1998 CD released in the United States. What is unique about this couple, apart from their shared marital status, is their com-mitment to creating an identity for Liberian music in the United States. Together with Joe Woyee, they established Kinzo Music Works, a music stu-dio in Minnesota, to produce and market Liberian music. The aim was to revive a trend that was beginning to emerge in the 1980s but was disrupted by the civil war.

Possibly the best-known Liberian musician is Miatta Fanbulleh, whose music is well known across West Africa and even beyond. As the daughter of a Liberian ambassador, Miatta started life in a privileged home, and this endowed her with a good education and a cosmopolitan outlook. However, she could not develop her singing talent to its full potential partly because of the constraints of her conservative (Muslim) and elitist family background. But she went to the United States in 1968 to start a career that recorded a mix of successes and setbacks. With academic qualifications in music and drama from the United States, she returned to Liberia in 1974 to relaunch her career in Africa and Europe. She collaborated with the eminent South African musician Hugh Masekela, with whom she toured the United States in 1976, and she was a notable presence at the World Black Festival of Arts and Culture (FESTAC), which took place in Nigeria in 1977. For the next seven years, Miatta Fahnbulleh settled in England, but she returned to Africa, where she became an outspoken defender of the rights and interests of women and children. Her contributions to cultural and community development were duly recognized with her appointment in 1990 as a goodwill ambassador for the Economic Community of West African States (ECOWAS) and as the official goodwill ambassador of her native country, Liberia, a year later.

NOTES

1. Lester P. Monts, "Conflict, Accommodation, and Transformation: The Effect of Islam on Music of the Vai Secret Societies," *Cahiers d'Etudes Africaines* 95, no. 24-3 (1984): 338.

2. The discussion of this theme draws heavily on Bai T. Moore's "Categories of Traditional Liberian Songs," *Liberian Studies Journal* 2, no. 2 (1970): 117–37. The songs reproduced in this section were taken with minimal alterations from this source, which is gratefully acknowledged.

3. I owe the Gola and English versions of this song to Dorith Ofri-Scheps, "Bai T. Moore's Poetry and Liberian Identity: Offering to the Ancestors," *Liberian Studies Journal* 15, no. 2 (1990): 32–33.

REFERENCES

Bender, Wolfgang. *Sweet Mother: Modern African Music.* Chicago: University of Chicago Press, 1991.

"Culturalpartnerships.org–Hawa Moore," http://www.culturalpartenerships.org/ontour/hawamoore.asp, accessed May 30, 2005.

DjeDje, Jacqueline Cogdell. "West Africa: An Introduction." In *Turn Up the Volume: A Celebration of African Music,* ed. Jacqueline Cogdell DjeDje. Los Angeles: Fowler Museum of Cultural History, 1999, pp. 140–68.

"Joe Woyee," http://www.cla.umn.edu/twocities/rprojs/Liberian.asp, accessed May 30, 2005.

Maxwell, Heather A. "West Africa: When the Xylophone Speaks." In *Turn Up the Volume: A Celebration of African Music,* ed. Jacqueline Cogdell DjeDje. Los Angeles: Fowler Museum of Cultural History, 1999, pp. 58–67.

Monts, Lester P. "Conflict, Accommodation, and Transformation: The Effect of Islam on Music of the Vai Secret Societies," *Cahiers d'Etudes Africaines* 95, no. 24-3 (1984): 321–42.

———. "Social and Musical Responses to Islam among the Vai during the Early Twentieth Century," *Liberian Studies Journal* 15, no. 2 (1990): 108–24.

———. "Ritual, Lore, and Music in the Pre-Islamic Vai Funerary Sequence," in *Turn Up the Volume: A Celebration of African Music,* ed. Jacqueline Cogdell DjeDje (Los Angeles: Fowler Museum of Cultural History, 1999), pp. 78–89.

———. "Islam in Liberia," in *The Garland Handbook of African Music,* ed. Ruth M. Stone (New York: Garland, 2000), pp. 51–73.

Moore, Bai T. "Categories of Traditional Liberian Songs," *Liberian Studies Journal* 2, no. 2 (1970): 117–37.

"Music of Liberia biography.ms," http://www.biography.ms/Music_of_Liberia.html, accessed May 30, 2005.

Schmidt, Cynthia. "Kru Mariners and Migrants of the West African Coast." In *The Garland Handbook of African Music,* ed. Ruth M. Stone. New York: Garland, 2000, pp. 94–106.

Stone, Ruth M. "A Musical-Dramatic Folktale of the Kpelle," *Liberian Studies Journal* 4, no. 1 (1971–72): 31–46.

"A World in Two Cities: Kinzo Music Works," http://www.cla.umn.edu/twocities/ rprojs/Liberian.asp, accessed May 30, 2005.

Glossary

Aladura A Christian denomination meaning "those who pray" (in Yoruba, a language spoken mainly in western Nigeria).

Alhadj Muslim who has made the pilgrimage to Mecca and Medina.

Anyun juwa de Weavers (Gola).

Bala Xylophone (Kpelle).

Bilite Traditional bone healer or orthopedic physician (Manding).

Blokila A mask with two projecting cow horns.

Bogaa Indigenous rice (Kru and Bassa).

Boo Flute (Kpelle).

Boubou Women's large and loose dress shaped like a gown.

Bugle Type of Dan mask.

Cire perdu Lost wax method of brass casting.

Dandai Major forest spirit behind Poro (Loma and Bandi); see *Landa/ Landai*.

Deangle Type of Dan mask.

Dendia Secular songs (Dei).

Du Tutelary spirit or spirit helper, the force behind every creature (Dan equivalent of *neme*).

Dudane Lesser spirits.

Fanga/tandegi Musical instrument for producing martial music (Belle).

Foofoo Popular dish derived from processed cassava.

Gbo Funeral dirges (Gio).

Gihn Talking drum.

Gle   Powerful forest spirits believed to empower masks (Dan/Gio).

Gle va   Great *gle* (Dan mask).

Ifa mo   Secrecy; literally, "do not speak it".

Jinaa   Spirits.

Jollof rice   Delicious rice dish; an amalgam of white rice and various condiments popular throughout West Africa.

Kamba/Kangmba   Supreme Being (Vai).

Kanya/Kanyah   Delicious snack produced from rice, peanuts, and sugar.

Karamoko   Muslim cleric.

Kembe   Literally, uncle (music instructor for the Poro, male counterpart of *kengai*).

Kengai   Vai women who supervise Sande musical activities; music and dance experts.

Kolako or Baa   Secular songs (Bassa).

Kongoma   Indigenous hand piano.

Kpokpo   Indigenous cloth.

Kuu (or demu)   Gio cooperative work group.

Kwii   Western or modern.

Landa/Landai   Major forest spirit behind Poro (see *dandai*).

Lappa   Wrapper (women's garment wrapped round the waist and legs).

Lemgbe   Secular songs (Gola).

Lime   Carved wooden human figures.

Mabole   Women of great spiritual influence (Mende).

Ma go   Small masks, called passport masks (Dan).

Ma/ma kpon   A popular game played with seed of the *ma* vine (Dan).

Meni-pelee   Musical-dramatic folktale of the Kpelle.

Moriman   Muslim spiritualists.

Negba   Taboos or conventions governing artists' relationship with their *neme*.

Neme   Artists' tutelary spirit or spirit helper (Gola and Vai).

Ramadan   One-month mandatory Muslim fast.

Sasaa   gourd rattle (Vai).

Shirk   Islamic fundamental doctrine of monotheism.

Sowei   Masks with high-ridged hairstyle.

Stepi   Cloth design consisting of a set of steps.

Suku   Vai Muslim musical genre (from Arabic *shukran*, to give thanks).

Suku-ba   Muslim musician (Vai).

Tan   Dance song (Gio).

Tombo   Dance (Vai).

Tuku   Wooden drum (Kru).

Turu   Side-blown horn (Kpelle).

Vai *keseng*   A real Vai person.

Vai *kpolo* Vai book.

Waya Secular song (Palipo).

Weplirkirgle Fun-making *gle* (Dan mask).

Wunkirlone or wunkade; singular, wunkirle Women honored for generosity (Dan).

Wunkirmian or wake mia Ceremonial ladle (Dan).

Yala Supreme Being (Kpelle).

Yombo Secular songs (Gio).

Yun maku he Wood carver (Gola).

Yun yai ene Tailor ("one who sews things" in Gola).

Zlan God (Dan).

Zloo Praise song (Gio).

Zo A Poro high priest (plural, *zoes*).

Zonga Powerful medicine men (Kpelle).

Zooba Masked dancer in the Sande society, impersonator of male ancestor water spirit.

Index

Aladura, 29

Allen, C. William, 41, 58

American Colonization Society, 1, 5, 10

Americo-Liberians, 4, 5, 13, 19, 22, 25, 28, 33, 35, 36, 38, 47, 74, 75, 80, 85, 111, 113, 119, 128, 140

Architecture and housing, 59, 61, 63, 65, 67, 69, 73, 74, 75, 77, 78

Art, carving/carvers, 59, 61, 62, 63, 64, 65, 66, 67, 68, 69, 70, 71, 73, 74, 75, 77, 78, 87, 90, 121, 138

Bandi, 3, 9, 22, 25, 35, 61, 85, 89, 92, 129, 131. *See also* Gbandi

Bassa, 3, 4, 5, 9, 10, 11, 25, 34, 43, 44, 46, 58, 74, 81, 89, 93, 131, 136, 141

Belle (Kuwaa), 9, 25, 93, 94, 119, 122, 123, 124, 126, 138

Bledsoe, Caroline H., 39, 107

Blyden, Edward W., 48, 50

Bomi (Tubmanburg), 5, 6, 16, 47

Bong, 5, 6, 13, 16, 46

Boone, Sylvia Ardyn, 77, 90

Brass casting, 67, 68, 69

Bride price, bridewealth, 66, 92, 93, 94, 96, 97

Brooks, Angie, 105, 106

Buchanan, 5

Bukele, Momolu Dualu, 44, 134

Bush devil, 9, 24, 25, 26, 27, 30, 33, 34, 37, 39, 60, 61, 63, 72, 85, 89, 94, 99, 116, 117, 121, 122, 129, 135–37, 138, 139. *See also* Poro

Cassava, 7, 48, 80, 81, 82, 83, 99, 100, 101, 131

Christianity, 21, 22, 24, 27, 28, 30, 31, 33, 35, 36, 37, 45, 48, 62, 91, 98, 117, 122, 127

Civilized, 25, 38, 79, 85, 86, 91, 98, 100, 101, 111, 112, 113, 120. *See also* Kwii

Class, 19, 27, 29, 68, 80, 98, 101, 105, 110, 112, 113, 119, 126, 140

Conteh, Al-Hassan, 39, 90, 126

Crafts, 4, 59, 77, 78, 90

Cuisine, 79, 80, 81, 83, 84, 85, 87, 89, 90, 109

Cuttington College, 4, 5, 6

Dalby, David, 58

Dan, 9, 60, 61, 62, 63, 64, 65, 66, 67, 68, 69, 70, 77, 78, 89, 90, 128. *See also* Gio

Dan Masks, 70

Dance, 65, 109, 127, 128, 129, 131,
132, 133, 135, 136, 137, 138, 139,
140, 141, 142, 143, 145

David, Soniia, 91, 107, 126

Daynuah, Jake (Jake D), 142, 143

D'Azevedo, Warren L., 77

Dei, 3, 9, 10, 129, 131, 134, 135

Dendel, Esther Warner, 78, 90

Doe, Samuel K., 2, 5, 14, 15, 16, 18, 23,
24, 30, 54, 55, 105, 106, 115, 120

Dress, 35, 41, 45, 68, 71, 79, 80, 81,
83, 84, 85, 86, 87, 89, 109, 111,
112, 118, 133; indigenous, 71, 112;
Western, 85, 86, 112

Du (Dan), tutelary spirit, 24, 26, 61,
62, 65, 66

ECOMOG, 2, 15, 16

ECOWAS, 2, 15, 16, 18, 144

Education, 4, 5, 13, 44, 51, 104, 105,
106, 107, 110, 111, 113, 116, 117,
118, 143; formal, 28, 31, 32, 35,
42, 43, 62, 98, 101, 102, 117;
indigenous, 130; Islamic, 32,
43, 117

Ellis, Stephen, 21, 39

Etiquette, 116, 119

Fahnbulleh, Fatima Massaquoi, 101,
104, 105, 107

Fahnbulleh, Miatta, 142, 143

Fernando Po, 52, 132

Firestone, 12

Folktales, 45, 48, 121, 128, 129

Foofoo, 81, 82. *See also* Cuisine

Football. *See* Soccer

Fraenkel, Merran, 126

Freemasonry, 22, 23, 30, 36, 37

Funeral rites, 122

Games, 72, 121, 129, 130

Gbandi, 3, 9, 22, 25, 35, 61, 85, 89,
92, 129, 131. *See also* Bandi

Gbarnga, 5, 6, 34, 75

Gender, 49, 62, 65, 91, 92, 93, 95, 97,
99, 100, 101, 102, 103, 105, 107,
113, 126, 129

Gio, 3, 9, 24, 26, 34, 60, 64, 70,
128, 129, 130, 131, 135, 141.
See also Dan

Gola, 3, 9, 10, 11, 22, 25, 35, 43, 47,
59, 60, 61, 62, 63, 64, 71, 72, 74,
77, 85, 86, 89, 93, 121, 129, 131,
132, 133, 135, 139, 141, 144

Grand Bassa, 5, 11

Grand Cape Mount, 16

Grand Gedeh, 13, 16, 132, 136

Grand Kru, 16

Grebo, 3, 9, 11, 25, 28, 37, 43, 92, 93,
100, 122, 129, 130, 138

Greenville, 5, 142

Hairstyles, 66, 70, 88, 89

Harper (Cape Palmas), 4, 5, 6, 28

Holsoe, Svend, 39, 78, 126

Initiation rites, 89, 93, 99, 116, 117,
121, 129, 135, 136, 137, 139, 142

Islam, 21, 22, 27, 32, 33, 34, 35, 36,
39, 42, 43, 45, 48, 50, 62, 85, 96,
98, 101, 117, 122, 123, 126, 127,
138, 139, 144

Johnson, Jangaba S.M., 45, 48, 126

Johnson, Prince Yormie, 5, 16, 121

Johnson-Sirleaf, Ellen, 17, 105, 106

Jollof rice, 80, 83

Karamoko, 32, 42, 43

Kissi, 3, 9, 43, 60, 71, 72, 85, 96

Konneh, Augustine, 39, 58

Kpelle, 3, 4, 9, 25, 27, 28, 32, 34, 35,
39, 42, 43, 46, 58, 74, 83, 91, 92,
93, 95, 96, 99, 103, 104, 107, 111,
112, 116, 117, 123, 126, 128, 129,
136, 137, 141, 145

Krahn, 3, 4, 93

Kru, 3, 9, 11, 12, 16, 81, 113, 114,
  128, 129, 131, 138, 140, 141, 145
Kwii, 38, 120. *See also* Civilized

Ladles, ceremonial, 65, 66, 69
Lappa, lappalonians (wrapper), 73, 79,
  85, 86, 88, 112
Ldamie, 67, 69, 70
League of Nations, 12, 52
Leisure, 88, 110, 114
Leopards, Leopard Society, 24, 26,
  121, 123, 124, 134, 138. *See also*
  Totems
Levy, Patricia, 19, 78
Liberian pidgin, 104, 110, 113
Liberians United for Reconciliation
  and Democracy (LURD), 6, 18
Literature, Liberian, 42, 47, 48, 49, 50
Lofa, 13, 16, 35, 119, 120, 130, 136
Loma, 3, 4, 9, 25, 28, 33, 42, 43, 46,
  58, 61, 89, 96, 116, 134, 138, 141

Mandingo, 3, 4, 10, 16, 22, 25, 32,
  33, 34, 35, 39, 42, 71, 85, 87, 96,
  117, 141
Maryland County, 6, 50
Masonic Lodges, 22, 23, 30, 36, 37,
  119. *See also* Freemasonry
Media, Liberian, 4, 41, 43, 50, 53, 55,
  56, 57, 58, 113, 125
Mende, 3, 9, 25, 58, 60, 71, 72, 77,
  88, 89, 90, 99, 104, 129, 135, 139
Monrovia, 2, 4, 5, 6, 10, 15, 16, 18,
  24, 25, 29, 31, 33, 35, 41, 49, 51,
  55, 74, 75, 76, 77, 86, 101, 102,
  103, 109, 110, 111, 112, 114, 126,
  140, 142, 143
Monts, Lester P., 144
Montserrado (also Mesurado), 5, 10,
  11, 12, 111
Moore, Bai Tamia Johnson, 47, 48, 49,
  107, 126, 141, 144
Moore, Hawa Daisy, 142, 144
Moran, Mary H., 91, 107, 126

Music: indigenous, 31, 121, 128, 135,
  136, 137, 138, 141; Islamic, 139,
  140; modern, 128, 140
Musical Instruments, 63, 138, 139
Muslim clerics, 32, 33, 42, 43, 117. *See
  also* Karamoko

National Patriotic Front of Liberia
  (NPFL), 15, 16, 17, 18, 26
Negba, 61. *See also* Dan
Neme, 24, 26, 61, 62, 63, 65, 66, 72.
  See also Du; Gola
Never-die Christians, 36. *See also*
  Sleboe, Richard K.
Newspapers, 44, 50, 51, 52, 53, 54,
  55, 56, 57, 115, 118. *See also* Press
Nimba, 13, 15, 16, 26
Nyei, Mohammed B., 41, 58

Occupation, 11, 118, 129
Ofri-Scheps, Dorith, 58, 107, 109,
  126, 144

Palipo, 131, 132, 136
Pentecostal Christians, 31
Peoples Redemption Council (PRC),
  14, 15
Perry, Ruth, 17, 105
Pidgin, Liberian, 4, 49, 104, 110, 113
Political culture, 109, 124, 125, 126
Poro, 9, 24, 25, 26, 27, 30, 33, 34, 37,
  39, 60, 61, 63, 72, 85, 89, 94, 99,
  116, 117, 121, 122, 129, 135, 136,
  137, 138, 139. *See also* Bush devil; Vai
Press, Liberia, 11, 41, 44, 50, 53, 54,
  55, 56, 57, 58, 115. *See also*
  Newspapers
Prestige, 9, 10, 46, 60, 61, 66, 71, 99,
  107, 118

Quiwonkpa, Thomas, 15, 55
Quran, 34, 42, 43, 45, 117, 140. *See
  also* Islam
Quranic education, 35, 43

Religion: Christianity, 21, 22, 24, 27, 28, 30, 31, 33, 35, 36, 37, 45, 48, 62, 91, 98, 117, 122, 127; indigenous, 22, 26, 27, 29, 33, 117; Islam, 21, 22, 27, 32, 33, 34, 35, 36, 39, 42, 43, 45, 48, 50, 62, 85, 96, 98, 101, 117, 122, 123, 126, 127, 138, 139, 144
Religion and medicine: and state, 38, 39, 90, 126
Revolutionary United Front (RUF), 2
Rice, 7, 9, 38, 65, 66, 69, 73, 79, 80, 81, 82, 83, 84, 92, 94, 95, 99, 100, 101, 116, 121, 122, 123, 129, 130, 131,135, 139, 141
Roberts, Joseph Jenkins, 28, 36, 74
Robertsport, 47
Rogers, Sr., Momo K., 58
Roye, E. J., 51, 75, 111

Sande, 9, 25, 27, 30, 37, 39, 49, 60, 61, 63, 89, 93, 99, 105, 116, 117, 121, 122, 129, 135, 136, 137, 138, 139, 142
Sankawulo, Wilton, 49
Sanniquellie, 5, 6
Sasaa, 138, 139
Saunders, Janice M., 91, 106, 107
Scripts, indigenous, 34, 43, 46, 58
Sherman, Mary Antoinette Brown, 105
Sierra Leone, 2, 3, 10, 16, 17, 18, 22, 58, 60, 73, 77, 78, 86, 90, 104, 113, 114, 128, 140
Sinoe, 5, 6, 11, 16, 36, 111, 142
Sleboe, Richard K., 36
Smyke, Raymond J., 107
Soccer, 71, 106, 114, 115, 116
Socialization, 64, 103, 110, 116, 117, 118, 121, 125, 130
Somah, Syrulwa, 79, 90
Sokay, Naser, 142, 143
Sowei (mask), 60, 89, 90
Spirits, 21, 24, 25, 26, 27, 33, 38, 65, 97, 103, 104

Sports. See Soccer
Status. See Prestige
Stone, Ruth M., 58, 144, 145

Taboos, 61, 81, 94, 104, 123, 124
Taylor, Charles Ghankay, 2, 5, 8, 15, 17, 18, 37, 55, 56, 106, 107
Tolbert, William R. Jr., 13, 14, 23, 24, 28, 30, 37, 38, 49, 53, 81, 85, 105
Totems, 24, 123
Traditional marriage, 92, 93, 95, 97
True Whig Party, 14, 22, 51, 52, 111
Tubman, William V.S., 6, 13, 23, 28, 30, 38, 48, 53, 85, 105, 111, 132

United Liberation Movement for Democracy in Liberia (ULIMO), 16
United Nations, 2, 48, 105, 106
United States, 1, 4, 5, 10, 14, 15, 22, 28, 37, 38, 44, 47, 48, 49, 50, 81, 104, 105, 113, 115, 118, 142, 143
University of Liberia, 4, 5, 15, 44, 45, 49, 57, 75, 105
Urbanization, 101, 110

Vai, 3, 4, 9, 10, 22, 25, 27, 32, 33, 34, 35, 39, 41, 42, 43, 44, 45, 46, 47, 49, 50, 58, 60, 62, 71, 72, 85, 89, 92, 96, 101, 104, 105, 107, 121, 123, 126, 127, 129, 130, 132, 134, 135, 138, 139, 140, 141, 142, 144

Weah, George, 106, 114, 115
Weaving, 9, 59, 71, 72, 73, 77, 78, 85, 90, 116
Wesley, Patricia Jabbey, 49
Witchcraft, 25, 67, 122
Worldview, 21, 22, 23, 24, 25, 26, 27, 31, 38
Woyee, Joe, 142, 143, 144

Yekepa, 5, 6

Zlan, 61, 68, 69
Zoo/Zoo-ba, 5, 9, 137, 139